MODERN HUMANITIES RESEARCH ASSOCIATION

CRITICAL TEXTS

VOLUME 17

Editor
JOHN BATCHELOR
(*English*)

THE REWARDE OF WICKEDNESSE

by

Richard Robinson

THE REWARDE OF WICKEDNESSE

by

Richard Robinson

Edited by

Allyna E. Ward

MODERN HUMANITIES RESEARCH ASSOCIATION
2009

Published by

The Modern Humanities Research Association,
1 Carlton House Terrace
London SW1Y 5AF

© The Modern Humanities Research Association, 2009

Allyna E. Ward has asserted her right under the Copyright, Designs and Patents Act 1988 to be identified as the author of this work.

All rights reserved. No part of this publication may be reproduced, stored in a retrieval system, or transmitted, in any form or by any means, electronic, mechanical, photocopying, recording or otherwise, without the prior permission of the publishers.

First published 2009

ISBN 978 0 947623 85 2

ISSN 1746-1642

Copies may be ordered from www.criticaltexts.mhra.org.uk

For Franklyn

TABLE OF CONTENTS

Introduction 1
Note on the Text 12
Abbreviations 13

THE REWARDE OF WICKEDNESSE

The Epistile Dedicatorie 17
The Author to the Reader 20
The Author to the Booke 22
The Booke to the Author 24
Richard Smith in praise of the Author 26
The Prologue 28
Helen of Troy 37
Newes between the Pope & Pluto 48
Medea 58
Pope Alexander VI 69
Heliogabalus 84
Tarquin 96
Tantalus 102
Turinus 116
Two Judges of Susanna 127
Pope Joan 136
Midas 144
Rosamond 150
To Noble Helicon 160

Bibliography 175

INTRODUCTION

Richard Robinson's lengthy poem *The Rewarde of Wickednesse* (1574) begins by establishing a winter setting for the poet's night of drinking that eventually leads to his journey into Hell with the god Morpheus. He begins, 'In December when daies be short and colde' before telling the reader that he wandered into a pub and proceeded to enjoy Ale with a jolly crowd: 'Some reeled, some fell, some helde them by the wall, / Some sang, some chid, and sware gogs precious bones'. Robinson continues to drink with this crowd until closing time when they all search for a place in the tavern to rest for the night and fall into a drunken slumber. However, shortly after falling asleep, Robinson's rest is interrupted by the god Morpheus. The poem then details Robinson's journey into Hell with the god of sleep where he witnesses the eternal punishments inflicted on sinners in Hell. During his dream he meets eleven (in)famous sinners from myth and history who tell their story and offer a warning about sinful behaviour. The most common sins Robinson attributes to the fallen figures are, incidentally, sins normally attributed to the Catholic Church during this period of Protestant reform[1]: pride, ambition, whoredom and tyranny. Helen of Troy is punished for her lust and pride; Pope Alexander VI is punished for ambition, tyranny, deceit and necromancy; Young Tarquin is punished for pride and whoredom; Medea, for whoredom and murder; Tantalus, for tyranny, hypocrisy, ambition and envy; Heliogabalus is punished for tyranny, ambition and whoredom; Vetronius Turinus, the Roman emperor who replaced Heliogabalus, is punished for ambition, pride and tyranny; the two judges of Susanna are punished for tyranny and as false accusers; Pope Joan, allegedly a ninth

---

[1] As, for instance, John Foxe makes evident in his use of examples from the past to show Catholicism as the false faith in *Acts and Monuments of the latter and perilous days, touching matters of the Church, wherin are comprehended and described the great persecutions & horrible troubles, that have been wrought and practised by the Romishe Prelates* (London, 1563), STC 11222.

century female Pope who reigned between Leo IV and Benedict III, is punished for her ambition and deception; King Mydas is punished for his tyranny; and, finally, Rosamond, is punished for murder and pride. Only two of the figures discussed in detail are distinguished by their corruption of the true faith, Pope Alexander VI and the legendary Pope Joan, although as you can see from the list, many of the sins are linked with Catholicism (as a subversion of truth) and more generally with the idea of being false. In some instances Robinson concludes a section with an author's verdict identifying a moral to be gained from the sinner's tale.

At the end of the journey through Hell the poet and Morpheus are greeted in the heavens and Robinson is asked by the sisters of heaven to warn others about the terrible punishments that await sinners in Hell. The poem, often overlooked or even dismissed in literary criticism,[2] marks the shift in the English literary tradition between a Medieval, Catholic way for writing about the consequences of earthly sin, repentance and Purgatory, to a Tudor, Protestant and anti-Purgatorial tradition.[3] It is a poem deeply rooted in historical events of the Tudor period and the history of English Protestantism and aside from its important place in

---

[2] In 1950 Elizabeth Marie Pope made a link between Shakespeare's phrasing regarding the fear of Hell and its torments in *Measure for Measure* and Robinson's language in *The Rewarde of Wickednesse*. She associates these texts and argues, 'many Elizabethan theologians attempted to make mad the guilty and appal the free by insisting on the materiality of Hell and giving excruciatingly concrete descriptions of just the sort of tortures that so terrified Claudio' ('Shakespeare on Hell', *Shakespeare Quarterly* 3: (1950), pp. 162-164). Otherwise Robinson has only received passing mention in larger studies of Renaissance literature.

[3] The concept of Purgatory was not universally accepted and remained a problematic part of the teaching of the Church. In 1536 King Henry VIII's government introduced the Ten Articles, which clearly outlined the guidelines for English Christianity. Five articles concerned Church Doctrine and five concerned Church Ceremony. G.W. Bernard says, '[The Article concerning Purgatory] rejected "popish purgatory" with a further blast against papal pretentions. It insisted upon the need to put abuses away, characteristic of Henry's commitment to purifying reform [. . .] It did not offer an exposition of traditional teaching on the subject. But, in what almost seems a response to advocates of a more radically dismissive position, it nonetheless declared that prayers and masses for the departed were beneficial' (*The King's Reformation: Henry VIII and the Remaking of the English Church*. Yale University Press: London, 2007, p.285).

the English *de casibus* tradition,[4] the poem is significant in what it tells us about the changing face of English Christianity. In this lengthy poem (eleven books plus the prologue and preliminary matters) that imitates the style of *A Mirror for Magistrates* (1559, 1563), Medieval Catholic accounts of Saint Patrick's Purgatory,[5] and John Lydgate's *The Fall of Princes* (1494), Robinson explores the association between earthly sin and Hell. Robinson narrates his experiences in Hell in dramatic form, giving a voice to the damned and allowing them to finally repent for their sins, although, as he mentions, it is too late to alter their eternal fates. The poem uses the *de casibus* form and the wavering theology it articulates is indicative of the constantly shifting perspective in the Tudor period regarding matters of faith, repentance and salvation[6] (evident in part through the

---

[4] The term *de casibus* in literary history comes from Boccaccio's *De casibus virorum illustrium* [*On the Falls of Famous Men*] and the English adaptation of Laurent de Premierfait's 1409 translation of Boccaccio's work. In English the tradition as a form of writing tragedy developed from Chaucer's *The Monk's Tale*, in which the Monk explains that he will relate a series of stories about people who fall from prosperity into misery as a result of a twist in fortune. See Paul Budra, '*A Mirror for Magistrates*' and the '*de casibus*' *Tradition* (Toronto: Toronto University Press, 2000) for a fuller analysis of the tradition in its early English manifestations.

[5] The punishments for sin were described at length in various Medieval purgatorial accounts despite the volatility of the doctrine of Purgatory. From the twelfth century, Catholics in Europe identified a cave in Donegal as the pilgrimage site of Saint Patrick. The legend of Saint Patrick's descent into the cave was one of the most influential sources of writing about Purgatory in European Christianity and the earliest surviving account of Saint Patrick's descent is the Latin text, *Tractatus de Purgatorio Sancti Patricii* (c. 1180). It was translated into English in the 15th century. Jean-Michel Picard's edition, *Saint Patrick's Purgatory: a Twelfth Century Tale of a Journey to the Other World*, provides the most comprehensive literary and cultural history of the story (Four Courts Press Ltd: Dublin, 1985). For a scholarly analysis of different extant editions and their relationship to Medieval dream visions see, *Saint Patrick's Purgatory*, ed. Robert Easting. Easting reprints the Latin *Tractatus de Purgatorio Sancti Patricii* (c.1180-1184); three Middle English translations of the Latin text; a thirteenth century and a fifteenth version called *Owayne Miles*; and the popular fifteenth century prose version in English, *The Vision of William Stranton*. Easting shows that these are the chief Middle English versions of the visions at Saint Patrick's Purgatory (p.xix).

[6] On the duplicitous nature of English Protestantism under Elizabeth, Patrick Collinson says, 'No doubt Elizabeth was some kind of Protestant [. . .] But certainly not hot Protestant: she was no Calvinist, indeed her evident belief in some kind of real presence put her closer to Lutheranism. She habitually used old-fashioned Catholic oaths [. . .] which curdled the blood of hot Protestants. She was attached to images that hot Protestants wanted to smash' (p.116). See his chapter on Protestant reform in the British Isles in *The Reformation* (London: Weidenfeld & Nicolson, 2003) pp. 105-122. Also see Eamon Duffy, *The Stripping of the Altars: Traditional Religion in England 1400-1580* (London: Yale University Press, 1992, 2nd ed. 2005) pp.377-555. In his introduction Duffy reminds his reader of the complex acceptance of Protestant

combination of forms and traditions working within Robinson's poem). The poem is anti-Catholic polemic, but it is not simply an invective against Catholicism; Robinson's work condemns bad moral behaviour but in the context of the dialectical opposition between Catholicism and Protestantism, an opposition that was not clearly demarcated during this period.

* * * * *

The poet Richard Robinson, and author of *The Rewarde of Wickednesse*, must be differentiated from the contemporaneous compiler and translator Richard Robinson of London. We know very little about our poet Robinson, except that he was probably from Alton in Staffordshire.[7] In the preliminary matters of *The Rewarde of Wickednesse* he identifies himself as a servant for the Earl of Shrewsbury and he dedicates *The Rewarde of Wickednesse* to Gilbert Talbot, the Earl of Shrewsbury's second son. Edward Arber's records of the Stationers' Company (1554-1640) cites three texts attributed to Robinson from Staffordshire: *The Ruefull Tragedie of Hemidos and Thelay* (1569), sadly lost; *The Rewarde of Wickednesse*, first printed in 1573 although the printer's device at the foot of the colophon is dated May 1574; and *A Golden Mirrour* (c. 1587), also dedicated to Gilbert Talbot and published posthumously by John Proctor.[8]

In the four introductory poems: 'Author to the Book', 'Book to the Author', 'Praise of the Author', and the

---

doctrine that Robinson's poem, I argue, articulates: 'The religion of Elizabethan England was of course full of continuities with and developments of what had gone before. Even after the iconoclastic hammers and scraping-tools of conviction Protestantism had done their worst, enough of the old imagery and old resonances remained in the churches in which the new religions was preached to complicate, even, in the eyes of some, to compromise, the new teachings' (p.4).

[7] 'Robinson, Richard' (fl. 1573–1589)', Brian Cummings, *Oxford Dictionary of National Biography*, Oxford University Press, 2004 http://www.oxforddnb.com/view/article/23865 [Date accessed: 21 Feb 2008].

[8] *A Transcript of the Registers of the Company of Stationers of London, 1554-1640 A.D.* Edited by Edward Arber. 5 Vols. (New York, P. Smith, 1950).

'Prologue', Robinson prepares his readers for the material in the core of the poem and establishes his position as a minor author, but also a devoted Protestant. In the first poem he describes his purpose in writing and what he hopes to achieve by detailing the horrible rewards awaiting those who sin.

In the prologue for *The Rewarde of Wickednesse* Robinson establishes the sombre mood and tone of the poem and evokes the landscape of Thomas Sackville's winter journey to Hell with his guide Sorrow in the 'Induction' added to William Baldwin's 1563 edition of *A Mirror for Magistrates*. This image of death and the desertion of winter that Robinson describes at the start of his adventure in Hell draws our attention to the multi-vocal nature of his poem in the allusion to Sackville's journey to Hell and his description of the cold, harsh conditions of winter.[9] Sackville comments that while he was walking on a winter's night,[10] gazing at the sky, contemplating the sudden shifts in fortune that men endure and how best to warn people about the dangers of Fortune, he suddenly encounters the mysterious figure Sorrow and is struck by her piteous appearance and her tearstained face. Moved by her sickly appearance, Sackville beckons her to speak and at this request the figure identifies herself: 'Alas, I wretche whom thus thou seest distreyned / With wasting woes that never shall aslake, / *Sorrowe* I am'

---

[9] Thomas Sackville, 'Induction', pp. 298-317. *A Mirror for Magistrates*. (1559 & 1563). Ed. Lily B. Campbell. (Cambridge: Cambridge University Press, 1938).

[10] Alan T. Bradford recognises the convention of Tudor writers to embrace the dark winter landscape, not because it was the stuff of good poetry but because of its relation to the human condition: '[w]hatever the poetic virtue of Sackville's description, it is not to be found in the freshness or acuteness of his observations of nature or in the originality of his expressive vocabulary' (Alan T Bradford, 'Mirrors of Mutability: Winter Landscapes in Tudor Poetry.' *English Literary Renaissance* 4 (1974): pp.3-39, p.13). Sackville's purpose, argues Bradford, was to, 'give cosmic resonance to the *Mirror* tragedies by linking the mutability of human affairs to the ineluctable processes of nature' (p.27). He argues that Sackville was participating in a tradition for linking the cycle of the seasons with what he identifies as the 'postlapsarian vicissitudes of human life' (p.19). Bradford dismisses Robinson's winter landscape from this tradition because it does not meet the literary standard of Sackville's poem. But, by excusing Robinson's poem Bradford overlooks the developing tradition for writing about Hell in early modern England.

(pp.106-8).[11]   In his anti-purgatorial account of the 'rewards' for sin in Hell, Robinson's *The Rewarde of Wickednesse* sets up a dialogue with earlier texts such as *A Mirror for Magistrates* and earlier traditions in an attempt to definitively describe the inescapable punishments that await sinners in a firmly Protestant perspective for a modern Protestant audience.

For instance, Robinson furthers this intertextual dialogue, setting up a contrast between his work, *The Rewarde of Wickednesse,* and Ulpian Fulwell's popular comic interlude from the 1560s, *Like will to like quoth the Devill to the Collier* (first performed in 1562, published in 1568). The interlude focuses on the rewards of heaven to lure men towards virtue, rather than emphasising the punishments for sin. Fulwell's text identifies the rewards of good moral behaviour but also links earthly sin with the infernal. His depiction of this link offers a strong contrast to Robinson's poem that connects earthly sin with Hell by focusing on the rewards for wickedness.

After the god Morpheus reassures him of a safe passage through the wards of Hell, Robinson willingly accompanies the god of sleep into Pluto's kingdom. As they approach the second ward their path is blocked by Wrath, Envy, Pride and Whoredom, who are, Robinson tells us, 'monstrous and ouglie'. The dramatic characters in Robinson's list, including figures such as Oppression and Private Gain, recall those Sackville passes in the jaws of Hell ('Induction', pp.218-292) and the figures described in Virgil's throat of Hell in *The Aeneid* (VI.273-281).[12]   Neither Virgil nor

---

[11] Cf. Sackville's description of Sorrow recalls the tone of the opening verse of *The Consolation of Philosophy*: 'Allas! I wepynge, am constreyned to bygynnen vers of sorwful matere, that whilom in florysschyng [flourishing] studie made delitable ditees. For lo, rendynge muses of poetes enditen to me thynges to ben writen, and drery vers of cretchidnsse weten my face with verray teres' (Chaucer, 397).

[12] For Virgil, those punished in Tartarus are superhuman rebels and evil men, but Aeneas does not have any direct vision of their punishments. At Aeneas' request the Sybil explains that after sinners condemned to Hell have confessed all their crimes to Rhadamanth, Tisiphone flogs them until the Furies come to take the sinner further into Tartarus where they will be eternally punished. She describes the punishments of certain rebels such as Salmoneus, Tityos, Ixion, and Theseus, who offended the gods with their disobedience. When the Sybil comes to the mortals who are punished

Sackville propose that the origin of sin is in Hell and the figures representing the specific sins are located at the outer edges of Hell. Robinson's use of, and departure from, his models' topography asks the reader to re-evaluate the origin of sin and proposes that the infernal realm has some control over the fates of men and women.

Before they enter the place in Hell where sinners are actually punished, Robinson and Morpheus, like Thomas Kyd's Don Andrea in *The Spanish Tragedy* and Sorrow and Sackville in the 'Induction', must pass through an infernal court. The hierarchical structure of Robinson's Hell indicates that the infernal god has some control over the eternal fates of men and women in Hell (if eternal judgement is reserved until after death) and, further, that specific punishments for sin are not fixed before death. Robinson deviates from Sackville's placement of Pluto just past 'Rude Acheron' and 'Blacke Cerberus, the hydeous hound of Hell' ('Induction', p.480, p.499) by placing the infernal court in the core of Hell. The poems in *A Mirror for Magistrates* do not dwell on the punishments that await sinners, only on how sinners fall from grace, but Robinson's poem is concerned to show that the spectacle of Hell's torments is directly linked to a sinner's actions on earth and so the infernal deities work with the judge Minos to appoint punishments, alongside the king and queen of Hell.

The *de casibus* framework of the poem is immediately established on the title page, and his anti-Catholic agenda is brought sharply into focus by his identification of Catholic clergy as 'ungodly':

---

in Tartarus, she does not recall their names but only categorises them according to their crimes. Virgil was content though to leave most of the description of the punishments of Hell to this second-hand account from the Sybil, who concludes, 'Even if I had one hundred tongues and one hundred mouths, and a voice of iron, it would not be possible to capture all the types of crimes or to run through all the names of the punishments' (Translation my own). Robinson repeats this sentiment when he describes the allegorical vice figures in the second ward of Hell: 'Many thousandes there were that I omit, / For want of time fullie to describe, / To tell truth the number passeth skill and wit, / To be namde of mee, that howled there and cryde' ('Prologue', pp.169-172).

> The rewarde of Wickednesse: Discoursing the sundrye monstrous abuses of wicked and ungodlye worldelinges: in such sort set downe and written as the same have beene dyversely practised in the persones of Popes, Harlots, Proude Princes, Tyrauntes, Romish Byshoppes, and others. With a lively description of their severall *falles* and finall destruction. Verye profitable for all sorte of estates to reade and looke upon. Newly compiled by Richard Robinson
>
> (*The Rewarde of Wickednesse*, t.p., emphasis my own).

The title is complemented with a brief caveat that points the reader in the direction of tragedy: 'A dreame most pitiful, and to be dreaded' (t.p.). All of the key words that Robinson draws to the reader's attention on the title page (especially: monstrous, ungodly, wicked, pitiful, dreaded and strange) point to the polemical nature of his *de casibus* poem because of their association, in the early modern period, with anti-Catholic propaganda. Mark Thornton Burnett discusses the significance of *monstrous* shapes and forms in the theatres, fairgrounds and exhibition spaces in the sixteenth century in his *Constructing 'Monsters' in Shakespearean Drama and Early Modern Culture* and shows how characteristics that deviated from the boundaries of what was considered normal were monstrous. The term 'monster' was used to describe people, actions and social practices which were considered unnatural and Burnett demonstrates that some even thought that monsters, or unnatural appearances, indicated the presence of sin: 'monsters [. . .] owed their conception to sin, with the *monstrous* actions of the parents being reproduced in the *monstrous* shapes of their progeny'.[13]

---

[13] Mark Thornton Burnett, *Constructing 'Monsters' in Shakespearean Drama and Early Modern Culture*. (Palgrave: Basingstoke, 2002) p. 26.

Furthermore, Burnett states, things that were monstrous were also considered devil-like and this was sometimes emphasised with the word 'strange', which was generally applied to matters of faith. In trying to determine the causes of types of 'monstrous' shapes, early modern writers maintained that 'monsters' were the result of Godly interference, and even devilry: 'The myriad arguments that 'monsters' were the result of bestiality, copulation during menstruation, devilry, incest [. . .] posit a relationship between a transgression of godly injunctions and the precipitation of dire parturient consequences' (Burnett p.27). In Robinson's application of the words 'monster' and 'strange' to the examples of ungodliness and wickedness in the title, he places his dramatic poem in the developing relationship between ungodliness, monsters and damnation that will come to dominate the stage-tragedies in the 1580s and 90s (for example, *Doctor Faustus*, *Tamburlaine* and *Richard III*).

Robinson's application of the *de casibus* form and the examples' warnings about the rewards for sin place the accounts in a unique Elizabethan mirror tradition. The poem is a testament to the anxieties created by alternate ways of thinking about Christian doctrine in its failure to direct the reader to any definitive way for avoiding sin or damnation. Willard Farnham comments, '[Robinson] simply serves in his humble way as a sign of the fervour which the conception of tragic justice was beginning to arouse'.[14] Tyranny, it seems, goes hand-in-hand with damnation and at times Robinson uses the term interchangeably with sin. Towards the end of his journey we witness Pluto thanking some of the damned for bringing in more souls to Hell but he does not actually appear to appoint anyone to do this task. Robinson's link between earthly sin and Pluto is evidence of the shift in thinking about the origins of earthly sin. Furthermore, his link between Pluto and Bonner, Pope Alexander VI and Pope Joan, indicates a specific perceived connection between Catholics and Hell, although at times

---

[14] Willard Farnham, *The Medieval Heritage of Elizabethan Tragedy*. (Oxford: Basil Blackwell, 1963) p. 306.

Robinson is tentative about this relationship because it could suggest that there is an active and successful adversary to God. The poem's exploration of matters of sin and damnation in relation to Hell and Pluto acknowledge the relevance of these issues to an Elizabethan audience.

Robinson's poem *The Rewarde of Wickednesse* explores the notion that sinful people on earth are influenced by a Hellish force but he empasises the punishment for sin and makes the link between the damned and Hell. *The Rewarde of Wickednesse*, through its inclusion of different, and sometimes opposing, traditions, faiths and literary formats, reveals an Elizabethan culture rife with the apprehensions concerning salvation and damnation that define early English Protestantism.

* * * * *

The Rewarde of Wickednesse consciously imitates various popular publications of Robinson's day in both form and metre. However, as will be evident, the poet fails to consistently follow any particular style and the collection contains an assortment of different forms.

The preliminary materials, 'The Epistle Dedicatorie' and 'The Author to the Reader' are penned in Prose and the 'Author to the Booke', 'Booke to the Author' and 'Richard Smith to the Author' are written in rhyming couplets. The Prologue is written in rhyme/rime royal, normally septets in iambic pentameter: A B A B B C C, as in Chaucer's *Troilus and Creside* and *The Parliament of Fowls* and John Heywood's *The Spider and the Flie*. The first account, the history of Helen of Troy, like Chaucer's *The Monk's Tale*, is written in octets in iambic pentameter (except for the first line of the section, 'O Foulest fury, that raging hel doth guide', which is hendecasyllable) and concludes with an author's verdict, written in rhyming couplets. The account of Pope Alexander VI, follows this form but the rhyme scheme varies slightly throughout and it also includes the author's verdict, written in rhyming couplets. In total, only four accounts follow this formula: iambic pentameter octets with a verdict in rhyming couplets: Helen of Troy; Pope Alexander VI; Medea and Heliogabalus.

I believe these accounts were written around the same time as each other to be placed together at the start of the collection. The accounts of Young Tarquin and Tantalus are written in septets using the rhyme scheme A B A B B C C, as in the Prologue. Tarquin's account does not include a verdict. Vetronius Turinus (includes a verdict) and Pope Joan (no verdict) are written in sextets and follows the A B A B C C pattern, while the Two Judges of Susanna returns to the form of the Prologue in form and metre but includes a verdict that is addressed to the Judges. The account of Midas follows the pattern of the author's verdicts and is written in fourteen-syllable rhyming couplets without a verdict. The last account, the account of Rosamond, is written in sextets and does not contain a verdict.

Generally the form and metre of Robinson's text is inconsistent and fails to follow any organized pattern so it is difficult to determine Robinson's intention. This, we may feel, is one reason for the text's subjugation to the realms of minor Elizabethan literature and its relative obscurity.

NOTE ON THE TEXT

The manner in which the sheets are collated in the original copy of the 1574 manuscript of *The Rewarde of Wickednesse* held in the British Library suggests that Robinson, or the printer, did not place them in the sequence that was originally intended. This copy is printed in the following order: Helen of Troy; Pope Alexander VI; Young Tarquin; Medea; Tantalus; Vetronius Turinus; Heliogabalus; The Two Judges of Susanna; Pope Joan; Newes between the Pope and Pluto; Midas and, finally, Rosamond. However, reading the individual poems that make up *The Rewarde of Wickednesse* in this order constitutes a contradictory and often incoherent experience. There are, however, various references throughout the poem which demonstrate that Robinson was working to a more coherent general scheme. For instance, the interlude about a ladder to heaven starts, "Thus leaving Helen" but is printed towards the end of the poem even though the episode concerning Helen of Troy is placed first in the 1574 MS.

Therefore, in producing the first contemporary edition of the text I have chosen to slightly alter the arrangement of the different episodes to best mitigate the numerous inconsistencies obvious in the 1574 manuscript. Although in a certain sense any collation of the individual episodes of *The Rewarde of Wickednesse* is ultimately bound to remain subjective, some accounts clearly belong together, either because of the rhyme scheme and form or the content. The order of the accounts that I feel reflects a better unity is as I have collected them here: Helen of Troy, Newes between the Pope and Pluto, Medea, Pope Alexander VI, Heliogabalus, Tarquin, Tantalus, Vetronius Turinus, Pope Joan, the Two Judges of Susanna, Midas and Rosamond. The sequence that I have placed the accounts in is not intended to limit further speculation as to Robinson's intentions with the text. It is rather meant only to provide a readable printed version of this little known poem.

List of Abbreviations

OED	*Oxford English Dictionary*
	Online Edition
	http://www.oed.com/

OCD	*Oxford Classical Dictionary*, 3rd Edition Edited by Simon Hornblower and Antony Spawforth. Oxford: Oxford University Press, 1999.

DNB	*Oxford Dictionary of National Biography –*
	Online Edition
	http://www.oxforddnb.com/index.jsp

THE REWARDE OF WICKEDNESSE

The Rewarde of Wickendnesse

Discoursing the sundrye monstrous abuses of wicked and ungodly worldlings: in such sort set downe and written as the same have been by verily practised in the persones of Popes, Harlots, Proude Princes, Tyrauntes, Romish Byshops, and others.

With a lively description of their several falles and final desctruction. Theyr profitable for all sorts of estates to read and look upon.

Newly compiled by *Richard Robinson,* Servant in the household to the right honourable Earle of Shrovesbury.

A dreame most pitiful and to be dreaded

Of things that be strange,

Who loveth to read:

In this Booke let him range,

His fancy to feed.

THE EPISTLE DEDICATORIE

To the Woshipful, Gilbert Talbot,

Esquire, Second Son to the Right Honourable Earle of

Shrovesbury &c. *Richard Robinson* Wisheth the fervent fear of God, Increase of Virtue, Worship and Honour, with Good Success, and many joyful years.

For as much as the little creeping Creatures of the Earth, doe teache everie reasonable person to use some kinde of trade, whereby for his travaile in the Sommer, hee maye in the blustering blastes of Storming *Hiemps,*[1] be relieved by the sweate of his browes, when nothing else is to be reaped upon the soil, but only Monstrous and huge driftes of Snowe: Which is dayly put in use by the little *Dormous,*[2] who in the Sommertime ceaseth not from travelying, till shee be fully perswaded to have sufficient store in her Cabbin, to defende the hungry time of winter: Likewise the crawling *Ant*, toileth from the first showe of Sir *Phebus* face in the morning, till the blacke Mantelles doe obscure the blasing beames of the same: The *Squirrill* that lightlie Leapes from Braunche to Braunche, is ever occupied, as appearesth by the greate store of Nuttes, that shee heapeth together in Sommer time, to incounter the barren season: The fearefull Flye is not forgetfull of the same, but carrieth his travailes to the warme hollowe reede, wherein hee dwelleth wholsomely, and Bankettes[3] merilie of his late travailes: (What shall I say, of the busie Bee) whose curious skill in building of her Lodge, and knowledge in Flowers and Hearbes, in chosing

---

[1] Hiemps: winter.

[2] Dormous: Dormouse. The *OED* cites Roger Ascham's use of the word in the sense of a sleepy person in *The Schoolmaster* (1568): 'Any lurking Dorm[o]us, blinde, not by nature, but by malice'.

[3] Bankettes: banquets (verb).

the Good, and leaving for the Spider the ill, never ceasing, but alwayes in travaile, hoping in winter to rest and enjoye the fruites of her travaile: Immediatelye upon the sodaine, is not onelye spoiled of this the fruites of her great toyle, but commonlye slaine for the lucre therof: (Even so) Right Worshipful, as I am not onely taught to abandon Idlenes, as wel by the holy Scriptures, as also by these creeping Creatures: So am I doubtful, least after my travaile, I shall reape the harmeles *Bees* rewarde: Except, (as my trust is) your Worship do seeme by your curtesie, to protect as well mee, as this little portion of my labour: For mee thinkes that I heare already *Envie* whet his Teeth, whose blade woulde long agoe, have beene bathed in my blood, if secreate thwacks could have touched my guiltless Carkas: Yet not withstanding I see the blasing brond[4] in his fist, to heare the great *Cannons* upon me: for already falle *Report* his Trumpeter, soundeth up his forging Trumpe of Detraction, whose honest nature is neither content with that which hee wisheth him selfe, nor yet pleased if he might have or obtaine, that which other men desire. Many mo friends this chasing Champion hath, whose Cankered mindes, and prowde stomackes, would not much stick to take in hand to Lift with *Atlas*: To wrestle with Sampson, or to take the club from *Hercules*. But disdaining further to speake of *Envie*, and his saide friends, which hateth every man, and every man him, them, being nothing doubtful of M*omus*, *Zoilus*, nor *Sicophants* whelps:[5] I am as well content to beare with their barking, as many worthy Clarkes heretofore have done, and doe daylye. So that is maye please your Worshippe, to take in good part this simple travaile of mine, which to eschewe Idlenes, and speciallye in suche times as my turne came to serve in watche of the Scottishe Queene, I then every night collected some part thereof, to the end that nowe it might be better appeare, that I used not altogeather to sleepe: Though one time I chaunted among many watchful

---

[4] Bronde: Brand, i.e. a fire-brand, a torch.

[5] Momus is the god of satire; Zoilus was a Cynic Philosopher (400-320 BCE) known for his harsh cynicism; and the Sycophants were a group of Ancient Athenian informers although the word was also applied to deceivers and untrustworthy people in the sixteenth century (*OED* def. 2,3 & 4).

nightes, to take a slumber, which incited mee to compile this fiction of *Poetry*, as more largely appeareth in my *Prologue*: And though it bee a Dousie Dreaming peece of worke, neither gardished with *Rhetorike, Eloquence, Curious* termes, nor pleasaunt matter, to purchase prayse of daintie Dames, and fanastical Kinghts of *Cupid's court*: (As it is not painted with these properties) so I am assured that your worship doth not mislike the want thereof. And for that it was thus begunne and ended in my Lord your Fathers house:[6] my singular good Lord and Maister, for whome, and my good Lady my Mistres, I and al mine, dayly pray, as we are many waies bound to doe: Doe nothing mistrust, but that your worship will the rather take in good part the same, not weying the gift, but the good will of the giver. And so your worship doth as well binde me and mine, to reste yours, to our power, as also therby, my poore peece of travaile from the spoile of *Sclander*, and the blody butcher *Envie*, by the same, garde and keepe, for otherwaies, my saide enemies will not sticke to reward my paines with the poore harmles *Bee*. Thus I cease, and rest.

Your Worshippes poore beseecher, *Richard Robinson.*

---

[6] Robinson worked for George Talbot, the 6th Earl and father of Gilbert Talbot, the second son and 7th Earl. In 1568 Queen Elizabeth appointed George Talbot the jailer over her cousin Mary Stuart during during the period of her eighteen-year imprisonment when she was housed at Sheffield Castle and Sheffield Manor. At the end of this epistle Robinson indicates he wrote this letter from Sheffield castle in 1574.

The Author to the Reader

As Idlenesse the daughter of destruction, is to be abandoned of all me, that love to leade the life of good and honest members of a common wealth: so is it as conceient that every man yield account to his countrey of his Zeale and good wil that he ought by duty to beare unto the same, by some virtuous or Godly worke, for good example sake: In consideration whereof (Gentle reader) as well to profite my countrey (to my power) as also to eschew Idlenesse: I have attempted this my second worke[7] unto the place of thy indifferent judgement, not mistrusting, but thou wilt as thankefully accept the same, as I have willingly vouchsased to be: bestowe my travaile, to pleasure thy delite in reading hereof. And though it be escaped my handes, not altogether so wel plained and pollished, as I purposed it should have beene: Attribute I praye thee, the cause to the busie lives, that all my Lorde my Maisters men do leade in the service of our Soveraigne Lady, the Queenes Maiestie: Sith the protection of the Scottishe Queene was committed to my saide Lorde in charge, whose true and duetifull service therein, to his Prince both night and daie: as well by the travaile of his Honours owne Person, as also all them that serve him: I doubte not but *FAME* hath tolde it to all the Princes in EUROPE and noble subjectes: as it were to bee a Mirrour to the rest, that shall serve in credite of their Prince, from age to age, no litle to the encreasing of his honour, and all his: (which God maintaine). And I, being one of the simplest of a hundreth in my Lordes house, yet notwithstanding, as the order there is, I keepe my watche, and warde, as time appointeth it to mee: at the which times, gentle reader, I collected this together, faining that in my sleepe *MORPHEUS* tooke me to *PLUTOS* Kingdome in a Dreame: The which device, I mistrust not, but thou shalt thincke well of: Notwithstanding I knowe that the Papiste will gnashe his teeth at me: The wanton Dames will scolde at mee: The Covetous worldlinges will disdaine mee. The

---

[7] Robinson probably refers to the play, *Hemidos and Thelay*, (1569/70), mentioned in the Arber's *A Transcript of the Registers of the Company of Stationers of London, 1554-1640 A.D.*

vaine glorious personnes in Authoritie, will envie mee: False accusers will abhorre mee, Traitours will utterlye detest this my simple worke. Another sorte there is, whiche I namde not yet: As the Cobler, and *ZOILUS*: Whose nature is to plaie hissing *HIDRAS* parte, rejecting the vertuous labours of painefull personnes, Lying Idle them selves like Buzzing Drones, devouring up the sweete travaile of the busie Bees, (but for these I passe not).[8] Sithe the most noble and famous writers of the worlde, have not yet hitherto escaped the dint of their abhominable tongues. Wherefore I lothe lenger to bestowe the time so ill, as to speake of their beastlie behaviour against the skilfull. Beseeching thee once againe gentle Reader, that I maie reape at thy handes, but the reward of my good will, whiche shall not onelie content my travaile: But also binde mee another time, to present some other noveltie, more fitter to feede thy fantasie. Hoping in the meane while, thou wilt in my absence stande an indifferent friend. Thus wishing to thee and thine, as to my selfe and mine: I bid thee fare well.

From my Chamber in Sheffield Castle.

The xix of Maie, 1574.

Thy Friende, R. Robinson.

---

[8] Robinson places the cobbler alongside his second naming of the cynic Zoilus in his invective against the 'Papists' to whom his narrative is addressed in the earlier line: 'I knowe that the Papiste will gnash his teeth at me'. For this association of the cobbler and Ziolus he may be thinking of the type of condemnation against modern Catholicism such as in John Foxe's *Actes and Monuments* where Foxe says that 'Coblers do now heare confessions & minister the most blessed body of our Lord unto others' and also, 'Invideat Sathanas, & Zoilus iliarumpat, / Obtrectet mendax cum grege Roma suo / 'Let Satan cast a malignant look, let Zoilus burst his sides [with carping bluster], let mendacious Rome, together with its crew [i.e. all the pagan Latin authors] find fault.' (I thank Dr John Waś for his help with this translation). (John Foxe, *Actes and Monuments of these latter and perilous dayes, touching matters of the Church, wherein are comprehended and described the great persecutions and horrible troubles* (London, 1583), STC 11225.) This link with the corruption of Catholicism is further emphasised with the mention of 'busie Bees', a phrase Chaucer applies to women in *The Canterbury Tales* (the Epilogue to *The Merchant's Tale*) that Robinson appropriates here because of Chaucer's relation between business and deception : 'For ay as bisy as bees / Been they [women], us sely men for to deceyve' (Chaucer, p.168).

The Author to the Booke

Thy woefull plaints, thy rueful face, and carefull countenaunce shoe,
To all the worlde: bee not tonguetide, reveale abroade the woe.
That is among the sillie soules, in Plutos ouglie lake,
For wickednesse done on the Earth, howe Jove doth vengeance take.
Blushe not my booke, to thunder foorth, the tormentes thou hast seene,
Tell wilfull wits, and hatefull hearts, what just deserved teene:
In Plutos pitte they shall abide, that headlong plunge in sinne,
Bee not abashte to tell the best, what plagues be there within.
And whome thou sawe in sincke of sorrow, bewaile and toile in griefe,
Why and wherefore, for whome, and what, they bide in this mischiefe.
And why thou mournest, tell the cause, and wherefore thou art sad,
No doubt thy teares, and travaile both, may thousands make full glad,
Except the Cobler gin to carpe,[9] that alwayes loves to cavell,[10]
Or secte of Sicophants stur up, (Zoilus) that drunken Javel.[11]
To stampe and scorne against thy talke, that thou art chargde withall,
For to rewarde thy sugered gift, with bitter stinking gall.

---

[9] The Cobbler begins to speak.

[10] Allot (verb): to cast lots.

[11] Rascal.

(But if they doe) no force, no harme, their wonted use is knowen,
The difference both of them, (and thee) Report hath justly blowen.
And doubte not but the learned, love, thy company to have,
And hissing Hidras venimde stinge, shall daylie from thee save.
And when the skilfull heades shall scan, the tale that thou must tell,
I charge thee, pardon crave of them, it doth become thee well.
And if they doe demaunde, from whence thou came, or whats thy name,
The Just reward of wickednesse, my Lords I am the same,
(Saye thou) which came from Plutos Pit, whom Morpheus led with him,
In drowsie Dreame, to see the soules, Rewarded there for sinne.
Which sightes, so rare and seldome seene, as in my dreame I see,
Good Lords, and Ladies, with the rest, shall straight revealed bee,
And doing dutie, thus no doubte, but thou shalt bee imbraste,
Of suche as doe of honour, or of vertuous learning taste.

Quoth Richard Robinson.

The Booke to the Author

And must I needes be packing hence, about such newes to beare,
Which shalbe to the most, these daies, an inward griefe to heare?
Why knowst thou not, that worldlings wish, to dwel on earth for aie,
And may not bide, but them abhorre, which saye they must awaye?
Howe shall I scape the cruell Judge, that is corrupt with golde,
Or craftie Carles and Muckscrapes now, that al from poore men hold?
The Tyrant he will whet his blade, the prowde will present puffe,
The wanton Dames will skould at mee, the Roister strange wil snuffe.
Piers *Pickthanke* and *Tom Teltale,* will devise a thousand waies,
Tibbe Tittiuilly, that lowring Lasse, some yll on mee wil raise.
Whoremongers, they and al their mates, I doubt wil stone me straight,
Flatterers, Filchers, and *Sclanderers* both, I looke but when they sight.
Rent Rackers, that doe fleece the poore, and *Baillifes* false untrue,
With bragging *Officers* forgetting God, that Conscience bid adue.
Murder, Treason, Theft and *Guile,* maye not abide my face,
The greatest number at these daies, will hurt mee in eache place,
And lustie *Youth,* starke stamping mad, wilbe to heare these newes·
Wherfore I greeve these Dreames to tel, if it were in me to choose,
Thinkst thou theyle credit Dreames these daies, that Christ wil scarce beleeve?

No, no, I doubt it overmuch: then blame not mee to greeve.
But had thou pende some pleasaunt songes, of V*enus* smiling boye,
I not mistrust but almost all, would clappe their handes for Joye.
Or any thing, but that which doth, reproove mens silthy vice,
No doubt among the most, it would have beene of greatest Price.
But speede, as speede maye, abroade I will attempte in haste,
Eyther of thankes, or else rebukes, the tone or tother taste.
The vertuous sorte I not mistrust, the wicked here I warne,
The wise in christ, wil thanke me much, the foole wil laugh me scorne.
And now the paines & plagues below, where *Charon* rowes the barge,
As the aucthour hath commaunded mee, I shall declare at large.
And if I chaunse to speake amisse, thy pardon here I crave,
Repentaunce at the sinners hande, is all Christ seekes to have.

Richard Smith in praise of the Author

Ye Muses all of Thespyas, with sacred Songes that sing,
Now staie your steppes geve eare a while, and harke what newes I bring.
Your Sonne that lately did indite with sacred silver quill,
In Forest here is fled awaye, unto Pernassus hill.
Where hee among the Muses there, and Ladies of great Fame,
Contrites the time both daye and night, in service of the same.
Beholding of these Goddesse face, with bewtie shining bright:
Like to Diana with her traine, Resplendishing by night.
Ambrosia is his foode, sweete Nectar is his drinke,
What pleasures are not reaped there, that mortall heart can thinke?
I doe him deeme in deede, to bee sir Orpheus Fere,
Who made the stones to understande, and senceles Trees to heare.
The sauage Beastes of sundrye kinde, came thrusting in a throng,
And went out of the wilsome woodes, to heare his sacred song.
Suche grace the Muses geve to some, for to delight the eare,
And to allure the mortall mindes, enchaunted as it were.
A Diamonde for daintie Dames: For Peeres a precious Pearle,
This Robinson the Rubi red, a Jewell for an Earle.
Suche Pearle can not bee bought I knowe, for all the Golde in Cheape,
The graces heare have powrd their giftes togeather on an heape.
Suche giftes can not bee graft no doubt, without some power devine:
Suche cunning hyd in one mans head, as Robinson in thine.
If I might vewe thy pleasaunt Poemes, and Sonettes that excell,
Then shoulde I not thirst for the floodes of Aganippes well.

Thou profered prise at Olimpias, and gotte the chiefest game,
And through the schoole of cunning skill, hast scalde the house of Fame.
Where thou on stage alone, dost stande Triumphantlye,
About thy head a Garlande gaye, of livelye Laurel Tree.
Which that these Noble Nymphes thought good for blasing theyr renowme,
In token of this learned Lore, adorned with that Crowne.
If I should penne this praise, as thou doest well deserve.
It were a volume for to make, and time it would not serve.
For what needes water to bee brought, to powre into the Seas,
Or why doe I with Penne contend about this Robins praise?
Whome trumpe of truth hath blowen abroade, that hilles and Dales resoundes,
With Eccoes from the earth below, up to the skie reboundes.

Quoth Richard Smith, Clarke

RICHARD ROBINSON

The Prologue

In December when daies be short and colde,
And irksome nights amid the storms gan rore,
That flockes from feeldes forsake their folde,
And Birdes from swelling floodes do shrinke to shore,
The plowgh doth rest that cut the soyle of yore.
    And toyling Oxe in cabin close doth stande,
    That wonted was to travayle painefull lande:

And when the hawtie hilles and ragged rockes,
In mantels white be clothed rounde aboute:
When soules and beastes, aswell by heardes as flockes,
Seekes smoking springes, hote thirst to dowte,
Whose flames doth force the frozen bankes throughout,
    To yelde their flintish ribbes, to gusthing Hoods of raine,
    And locked streames at large to set again:

When everie Tree the ardent colours lost,
And brave depainted lookes of fragrant smelles.
When bragging *Boreas*[12] thus the soyle had tosst,
That Hart and Hinde[13] did quake in fieldes and felles,
With Bull and Beare for colde both cries and yelles.
    And shrowling makes eche thing that life doth beare,
    To stande with shaking limbes, the stormes to heare,

When eyther side the hilles when blasted doe rise,
As sharpe as thornes the naked skinne doth hit,
And *Saturne* to earth doth shewe his frozen eyes,
Which oft doth cause both young and olde to fall sicke,

---

[12] Boreas: The North Wind: brings winter.

[13] Hart and Hind: male and female deer.

With cough, and colde, and stopping rheumes also.
Quotidians, fevers, diseases many mo:

And when *Eolus*[14] his prison had unlocken,
And all the retchlesse route let runne at large:
Whose rushing rage eache pleasant braunch hath broken
Whereas before Dame *Flora* had the charge,
On *Tiber* stirreth neyther boate nor Barge.
    Trytan soundes hir trump, and *Neptune* gins to frowne,
    The sayler strikes from mast the sayles a downe.

When young and olde their bones with cloth doe loade,
And hoodes unto their heades doe buckle fast:
And when the Boye doth rest that bare the goade.
And keepes the chimneys ende til *Hyemps* storms be past,
When men doe doubt their winter stuffe to last,
    And carefull cattell with open Jawe doth crave,
    Their keepers meate their carkas for to save.

When men delight to keepe the fire side,
And winter tales incline their cares to heare,
When mery mates be met, that will abide,
Eache filles his pot of Nutbrowne Ale or Bere,
As is the trade of Ale knightes every where,
    To tosse the pottes and plye the flitting boules,
    Then pay their pence, and packe with drunken noules.

In this season it was my lotte to fall,
Among a masque chosen for the nonce,
Some reeled, some fell, some helde them by the wall,
Some sang, some chid, and sware gogs precious bones.

---

[14] Eolus: Servant to Juno and Ruler of the Winds who lived on Aeolia, an island near Thrace, where he kept the winds in a cave (mentioned by Virgil's *Aeneid* in Book I, ll. 50-85).

(Qoth one to me) friende camst thou from saint *Jones*?
>What penaunce hast thou done, thou art so leane & pale!
>No force (quoth another) he shall fyll his pot of Ale.

Content (quoth I) and therto I agree,
Fyll pot Hostice of Pery, Ale, or Bere:
My heade it recreated after studie,
To shut foorth the time, though rusticall they were
Thus walkt the Kanikin both here and there,
>Till the wife cryed to bed for saving hir fire,
>Contented (quoth I) for that was my desire.

The shot was gathered, and the fyre rakte up,
Eache man to his lodging began for to draw:
Some stackering stumbled as mad as a Tip.
Some crept under the mattresse into the strawe.
Another sort began to pleade the common lawe.
>I lookt about and sawe them so dight,
>Put out the candle and bad them goodnight.

My drowzie heart thus being at his rest,
Tooke no care for the colde, all sorrowes were past:
So late it had beene at the good Ale feast,
That the worlde for ever I thought woulde last.
In mine eare thunders no sounde of winters blast.
>I thought none yll, my heade was layde full saft,
>All carke and care my wandring sprite had laft.

Not lying thus one houre by the clocke,
Me thought the chamber shone with Torches bright,
And in the haste at doore I hearde one knocke,
(And sayde what) Slugge, why sleepest all the night?
I starting up behelde one in my sight,

Dasht all in golden raies before me did appeare,
(And sayde) I am a God, beholde that standeth here.

Mine eares were filde, with noyse of Trumpets sounde,
And dazled were mine eies, my sence was almost gon,
But yet amazde my knee vaylde to the grounde,
And sayde here Lorde, thy will and mine be one,
What is thy minde, more redie there is none,
    To ride to runne, to travell here and there,
    By land and sea halfe worthie if I were.

But first to know thy name I humbly thee beseeche,
Forgive my rudenesse this of thee to crave,
He aunswering sayde, with meeke and lowlie speeche,
Morpheus is my name, that always power have,
Dreames to shewe in Countrie, Courte, or Cave.
    In the heavens above, or *Plutoes* kindgome loe,
    Its I that have the power each thing t'unfolde and shoe.

And know (quoth he) that everie night and daye,
Who shutteth up his eye, his heade to feede with sleepe,
His wandering spirte attend on me alwaye,
To trudge and travell, where I shall thinke it meete,
As well to mounte the skies, as in the secrets deepe,
    As swifte as thought, what God hath greater poure,
    Then all that is or was, to shewe thee in an houre?

And whether wilt I goe, Lorde *Morpheus* (quoth I)
I here am prest thy will for to obey.
With an earnest lookes (quoth hee) I will that by and by,
To *Plutoes* kindome with mee thou take thy waye,
Though frayed I were, I durst not well say naye.
    With him I went that irksome place to see,
    Where wofull sprites full sore tormented bee.

And going by the way these wordes he sayde,
Be of good cheare, me thinkes though lookest pale,
Plucke up thy hearte and be no deale afrayde,
Although thou goe into this ouglie vale.
And thus or he had fynisht halfe his tale,
> *Cerberus* barckt that griselie hounde of Hell,
> The earth did quake to heare him houle and yell.

When *Morpheus* hearde this cruell barcking Curre,
For *Mercuries* rodde he sende with all the hast,
This wondering porter charmde he might not sturre,
Till hee and I throughout his office past,
So to the seconde warde wee came at last.
> Where *Wrath* kept the walles, and *Envie* the gates,
> Associate with *Pride* and *Whoredome* their mates.[15]

With cruel countinaunce terrible to see,
These horrible officers fixed their eyes,
Filthie to beholde monstrous and ouglie,
They gathered to the gates like swarmes of Bees,
Gnashing their teeth, asking who were these,
> That durst be so bolde *Plutos* kingdome to enter,
> Or within their office to rudelie to venter.

I am *Morpheus* (quoth hee) mine auctoritie you knowe,
As well in the heavens as also here,
My nature and qualities is dreames for to showe,
Therefore give place, and let me come neere.
These wordes scarce saide, but the gates opened were.

---

[15] Wrath, Envy, Pride and Whoredom, like Marlowe's pageant of the Seven Deadly Sins in *Dr Faustus*, are borrowed from the Morality tradition. For example, in *The Castle of Perseverance*, the devil Belial appears and reveals to the audience that he plans to destroy the soul of Mankind with help from his friends Pride, Wrath and Envy. In the next scene king Caro (Flesh) explains how he and his friends, Gluttony and Lechery, with his son Sloth, work to destroy Mankind.

So to the thirde warde we came by and by,
Not far from that place where great *Pluto* did lye.

The warde as I saide where *Pluto* then lay,
Was fortefied with Tirauntes for the nonce,
Some crying, sware yea, and other some nay,
Renting eche other flesh from the bones,
Some flang fiebrandes, and other some flange stones
    With howling and crying terrible to heare,
    What plague could be thought that was not present there?

The chiefe Captaines of all this rablous route,
Were *Opression* of the poore and eake *Private gaine*,
With a sorte of their kinne that looked full stoute,
That in that vale for ever must remaine.
There was Peter Pickethanke and Privie Disdaine,[16]
    Tom Teltale was appointed in a Turret to watche,
    Laurence Lurcher a Baylife to snatche and to catche.

There was *Darckenesse* and *Ignoraunce* linckt in a chaine,
With Errour and Freewill, Arrogance, and Selflove,
Forgetfulnesse of God, and Transgression did remaine,
With *Mistruste* and *Supersticion*, which might not remove[17]
Hipocrisie the King in a turret above.
    With *Lucre*, *Cruelnesse*, and *Bludshed* his brother,
    Domination, and Fulnesse, Abundaunce, and other.

Pompe he sat puffing as though here were madde,
Symony[18] under hade begane to convaye,

---

[16] Marginal Gloss: The greatest vices on earth be chiefe Captaines in Hell.

[17] Marginal Gloss: Let us abhorre these vices and cruell crimes.

Iniquitie and *Sophistrie*, with countenaunce full sadde,
Sat with *Murther,* and *Tyranny* cursing the daye,
Certainelie to see it was a tragicall playe,[19]
    To beholde abhomination, what torments she had,
    (with the rest) whereat *Confusion* was glad.

Many thousandes there were that I omit,
For want of time fullie to describe,
To tell truth the number passeth skill and wit,
To be named of mee, that howlde there and cryde.
When these lothsome leyds, had *Morpheus* espyde,
    They flew on heapes to know from whence he came,
    Who aunswered thus I am a God no man.

And whats thy name (quoth they) *Morpheus* aunswered he
Whome *Pluto* doth admire and honor both I trowe,
And *Proserpine* your Queene, mightie though they bee.
And *Mynos* your Judge will doe the same I knowe.
I am the God that always dreames doth show.
    I am free this waye to guide and leade eache man,
    Without demaunde to knowe from whence I came.

Then up start *Peter Pickethanke* by and by,
These newes to *Pluto* in haste he ran to tell,
And almost madde, with open Jawes gan crye,
My Lorde (quoth hee) thers Straungers come to Hell.
What else (quote *Pluto*) is not all thinges well?
    Yea Sir (quoth hee) its *Morpheus* that is here,
    Then *Pluto* aunswered, why bidst him not come neere?
The thirde warde opened then at large,

---

[18] 'simony': Forms: 3-6 symonye, -ie, (4 -i), 4-9 symony; 3-7 simonie (4 -ye), 6 simoni, 6- simony. 'The act or practice of buying or selling ecclesiastical preferments, benefices, or emoluments; traffic in sacred things. Freq. with initial capital', *OED*.

[19] Marginal Gloss: Confusion doth devoure wickednesse.

The Pallace then approching in our sight,
Where raging furies of wofull soules had charge,
To torment thousande wayes, both daye and night,
Miserable darckenesse there was without light,
    Grasping and groping greate discorde and strife,
    Weeping and wayling, and blaphemous life.

The stinking smoke that from that dungeon rose,
Corrupts the skies, and clowdeth all with shade,
The thundering blast that from the furnesse blose,
A dubble paine, the sillie sprites hath made.
With rufull plaints to heare in everie glade.
    That if the sorrowes halfe were pende I see,
    In teares there woulde be drowned manie an eye.

But when we came this ouglie God before,
Hayle (quoth *Morpheus*) thou God of darckenesse great,
Hayle *Proserpina* here Queene for evermore,
Long may thou holde thy place and seate,
I am come (quoth hee) my custome for to pleate,
    Thou knowest of olde that woont I am to see,
    As well thy kingdome, as mightie *Joves* on hie.

By *Styx* (quoth hee) thy auncient custome olde,
I will not breake, but as thou hast before,
In all my regiment, I will thou shalt be bolde,
To doe all thinges as tho wast woont of yore,
But looke of mee thou seeme to crave no more.
    Except you two, who is my gates within,
    To pray for pardon it profytes not a pin.

Then aunswered *Morpheus* I never thought to crave,
The pardon of the prowdst that in thy foyle doth rest,
Nor yet the greedie Tyraunt toombde in grieslie grave,

Nor any such that poorement hath opprest,
For gylefull gluttons to speake I thought it least.
    All these with other mo, I know must stay with thee,
    Howe wickednesse rewarded is all that I wish to see.

Content (quoth *Pluto*) and commaundment he gave,
To all his officers his kingdome through,
That *Morpheus* and I shoulde licence then have,
Eache place for to searche in Hill, Dale, and Clowgh,
In thick or in thin, in smooth or in rough,
    In hote or in colde where ever it bee,
    The wickeds rewarde we should both heare and see.

This saide, we departed from that filthie puddle,
And foorth wee past, the left side that cave,
Where wee founde a greater and crueller trouble,
Then all this while I knewe any to have,
For one among manie we hearde raile and rave,
    With a wofull voice me thought it saide this,
    Come see alas the rewarde of wickednesse.

At length to the place we chaunst for to hit,
Where *Alecto* had charge to rule and dispose,
There we behelde one lying in a pit,
Sodden is sorrowes from the toppe to the toes.
Their paines for to paine in meeter or prose,
    Doth pass my skill, the least to describe,
    Though *Tessiphon*[20] hir selfe my pen now shoulde guide.

---

[20] Allecto, Megera and Tisiphone, are the three Erinyes (gods of retribution and wrongdoing) identified by later Greek and Roman writers after Aeschylus such as Virgil. Virgil places Tisiphone at the gate of Tartarus, 'Tisiphone, swathed in a blood-dripping mantle, / Sleeplessly, day and night, stands permanent guard at the entrance' (VI.555-6). Virgil's Juno invokes Allecto to aid her plots against the Trojans: 'Thus cued [by Juno] Allecto set off, bathed foully in venom of Gorgons' (VII.341).

But what I sawe in this my drowsie dreame,
And who they were as now to minde I call,
Why and wherefore to you I shall proclaime,
That thus they lost the joyes supernal,
And have possest the wofull place infernall.
> Lend me your eares for now my tale beginnes,
> How wicked wightes rewarded be for sinnes.

Helen tormented for her treason to her husbande, and living in fornication ten yeares, whose wordes followe[21]

O Foulest Fury, that raging hel doth guide,
O worse then wrath, or endlesse wicked life
O swarming plages, ye passeth flesh to bide,
O doubtful dome of Plutos broiling strife.
O Stigion spew thy flames, to ende this life.
O just rewarde I saye, of wicked deedes:
O greatest mischiefe, among these puddels rife,
O come make haste, you flames of glowing gleedes.

You Gods that sit in seates of passing blisse,
> whose Joyes my endles paines surmounteth farre:
Doe you consent for to rewarde mee this,
> that whylome was in Grece, the Lampe, and Starre.
What meant you first to make and then to marre?
> I am the worke of all your whole consentes:
No brute nor fame, of Earthly woman harre,
> woe worth my fate, full sore it mee repentes.

---

[21] In Greek mythology Helen of Troy is the daughter of Zeus but Virgil says she is Tyndareus's daughter and fully human. She was the wife of Menelaus (king of Sparta) whose affair and abduction by Paris prompted the Trojan War. She was honoured for her beauty and later condemned because she willingly left with Paris. Virgil's Aeneas is cynical of her: '[Helen], a common demon of war for both Troy and her homeland [...] Flames were now rife in my soul, ire rose up within me, demanding / Vengeance for my dying homeland and summary, criminal justice' (II.566-88).

O worthye Dames, lende mee your listening eares,
    refraine your *Citherons,* and pleasaunt *Lutes* also:

With *Virginalles,* delighted many yeares,
    from out your heartes, let thought of Musicke goe.
Perhaps you daine, that I shall will you so,
    but mervaile not, ne at my wordes take scorne:
It is your partes though you were ten times moe,
    to helpe my plainte, with teares that I was borne.

Caste of your Golden Rayes, and ritche attyre,
    put on the mourners weedes, seeme to lament:
Hyde your painted faces, that sette mens heartes on fire,
    learne this of mee, your bewtye soone is spent.
You maye by mee your wicked lives lament,
    from spowting Conduites let gushe the sloods of teares
Let scalding sighes from broyled heartes be sent,
    your just rewarde for wickednesse appeares.

Although it doth abashe eache daintye Dame,
    to reade of me, or yet to heare me read:
I am the marke for you to shun like shame,
    disdaine me not though hygh you beare your head·
You that of Husbandes all this while be sped,
    bee true to them in all your conversation:
Beware take heede, defile no time theyr bed,
    among the Gods it's great abhomination.

I was in bewtye passing all the rest,
    and so by nature as curious made and wrought:
That if in me there had beene grace possest,
    to match the Gods I might have well beene thought.
But vertue is the bewtye, Ladies all,[22]

---

[22] Marginal Gloss: Vertue is the beautie of man and woman.

and not your painted faces and shining glee:
No greater mischeefe can among you fall,
   then for to feede your fickle prophane eye.

For once I had my selfe such prophane lookes,
   twirlde out with eyes that were celestiall like,
Whose sparckling twinche were sharper then the hookes,
   cast in the streame with baite for Fishe to bite
A thing immortall seemed I to bee,
    but yet corrupt with maners that were nought
As painted Tombe, with bones bee inwarde filthy:
   so outward I, but inwarde vices wrought.

And to her selfe be wayling thus alas,
   in eyther hande an Ore, shee laboureth sore:
At length shee was espide where I and *Morpheus* was,
   then calde shee us that stoode upon the shore.
Came neare good *Morpheus,* straight thee gan to rore,
   thou seest my paines, thou knowst not yet my name:
In *Stigion* lake I bide for evermore,
   the wife of *Menelaus* I am the verye same.

And *Helen* loe I am that heare abide,
   within this ryuen Boate, invironde as you see:
As just reward for fleshlye lust and pride,
   which escapeth not, but heare rewarded bee.
Many a worthy wight lost his life for mee,
   and dyed all berayde and covered all in blood:
Therefore I praye thee yet come neare and see,
   the tormentes I abide within this Hellishe flood.

Alas uneth my hande can holde the pen,
   my sight devoured is with greevous teares·
When I but thinke howe that I sawe her then.
   that once did leade the crewe of Venus apeares,
No honest heart but it would rewe her late.
   that hearde and sawe as much as wee that tide:
But all alas to greeve it is to late,
   the Gods ordeine that shee shall there abyde

Amid a Sea that boyleth fierye floods,
    with mixed blood flyes up and downe the Skies,
Where lurking Rockes with hautie dreadfull muds
    on everye side appeared in our eyes.
About the which moste venemous serpentes flyes,
    huge storming blastes this wicked streame doth move:
What sparkes of gleides rise up like swarmes of Bees,[23]
    and furies fell theyr wicked partes doe proove.

For in a Boate berent on everye side,
    (and as I sayde) shee sittes, in every hand an Ore:
And striveth styll betweene the winde and Tyde,
    nowe haling from the Rockes, and by & by from shore.
The choyse is harde, when this refuge is best,
    to toyle amid these flaming fluddes as shee:
Or else t'arive amid the Serpentes nest,
    for on the lande with blades the Tyrantes bee.

Which rounde about this plaguie Stigion pit,
    in battaile raye and armour blacke doe stande:
Cutthrotes, as egar as any Fishe of byt,
    that alwayes watche to see her come to lande.
Eache Butcher holdes a mortall Ore in hande,
    for to revenge the blood shee caused shed:
The which for truth, when as I vewde and scande,
    with heapes of woe, to *Morpheus* thus I saide.

Alas (quoth I) this greeves mee most of all,[24]
    to see her fate, whose bewtye Clarkes commende:
Mee thinke the Gods that sit in seates supernall,
    some mercye should at length and pitye sende.
Eache one (quoth *Morpheus*) who seemeth to offende,
    according to theyr deedes without respect

---

[23] Marginal Gloss: A discription of the place where she roweth in a riven Boate.

[24] Marginal Gloss: The Gods have no respecte of persons.

Have here rewarde for wickednesse in t'hende,
  as pleaseth *Pluto,* or whome hee hath elect.
And as these wordes were sayde, wee hearde hir crye,[25]
  (O *Paris, Paris,*) for evermore woe bee the time
Thy faigning face, it was my chaunse to spye,
  or that it was thy lucke to looke on mine.
Thou steynde my name, alas so did I thine,
  my mischiefe hit by thee, by mee the like thou had·
O wicked *Helen,* this all men maye define,
  And *Paris* for thy part, thy fortune was as bad.

O worthye *Troye,* happye had thou binne[26]
  if sleepie Nurse had strangled mee in bed:
Then bloodye mischiefe had scaped all my kinne,
  and noble *Hector* had never lost his head.
Many a worthy man had livde, that nowe is dead,
  Troy had florisht still, whose walles are sact full loe:
Menelaus had never yet polluted bed,
  and if the Gods my death had poynted so.

All *Greece* unto this daye, doth curse the time,[27]
  with many a famous Prince of noble birth:
So *Paris,* thou art like wise curst of thine,
  for thou and I were troubles to the earth.
Alas therefore nowe chaunged is our mirth,[28]
  the bloodshed in our cause doth vengeaunce crye:
Therefore take heede you Dames of mightye birth,
  to t'hende of all beginninges, ever cast your eye.

For, had I never painted up my face,
  nor shot the boultes of wanton whirling eyes:

---

[25] Marginal Gloss: The one, fornication destroyeth; the other, experience telleth.

[26] Marginal Gloss: What mischiefe doth not a wicked woman breede.

[27] Marginal Gloss: In ill bargaine wher no man innes. &c.

[28] Marginal Gloss: It is an old proverb take heede is a fayre thing.

RICHARD ROBINSON

Had grace and vertue dwelled in that place,
    then had I saved al the lives of these.
For when a man the lookes of women sees,
    hee lyeth at watche, to see her cast the darte:
Hit whome it happes, (hee is no man that flees,)
    then blame him not, that doeth defende his part.

For thou alas good *Paris* not to blame,
    (nor none but I) that cast my secreate lookes[29]
So sleightfullye, to tyse thee with the same,
    before the Gods I wish: none other bookes.
I caste him sugred baites, I catche on bitter hookes,
    or else the suite had *Paris* never take:
I layde him letters, in secreate holes and noukes,
    for to attempte the venture for my sake.

And what was hee that would not take in hande,[30]
    to hassarde all, at that time for my sake,
Whose matche on earth, did never goe nor stande,
    then blame him not suche enterprise to make?
O Ladies bee wittye, and quietnesse make,
    and dread the Gods you worthy Grecian Dames·
For here shee lyes within this flaming lake,
    bewrapt in woe, to quit her youthfull games.

My Pageant though I playde in open sight,
    and that the world did manifestly knoe:
I woulde not wishe that you by secreate night,
    or closer craft should use your Husbandes so.
The Gods above all sleightye secreates showe,
    to everye eare and eye, bee straight revealde:
You heare it read in Scripture long agoe,
    that naughtye actes were never yet concealde.

---

[29] Marginal Gloss: Old pleasure brede newe sorrowe.

[30] Marginal Gloss: Wickednesse destroyeth his selfe.

And then when Fame hath sounded up hir trumps,[31]
    and publisht all your deedes and filthy life:
Then shall confusion put you to your Jumpes,
    your Husbandes shall disdaine to call you wife.
Your friendes shall blushe to heare you namde,
    your foes rejoyce in every coast about:
To call you mothers, Children are ashamde,
    loe this besure, it ever falleth out.

And finallye the Gods from joye and blisse,
    shall cast you into *Stigion* lake to frye:
As pleaseth *Pluto* so your Sorrowes is,
    marke well my wordes, I doe alleadge no lye.
And then it is to late for to repent or crye,
    your woefull Scrikes rejoyseth Hell to heare:
(As for my parte) unhappye wretche I trye,
    whose juste reward thou seeist plaine appeare.

When fowlest thought of treason to your mates,[32]
    shall pricke your fickle mindes as some it doth:
Yet let this one thing pearce your peevishe pates,
    that like the slippie eyes so glideth from ye youth.
And sith there is nothing of greater trueth,
    through lewdenesse lose not then your noble names.
Bee most assured, mischiefe streight insueth,
    alas therefore, take heede you worthie Dames.

And scorne no deale, my rewfull plaintes to heare,
    if hap be on your sides, I maye such warning be
To everye one that is possest with feare,
    that by my fate lyke daunger for to flee.
Thesefore as ofte as follye feedes your eye,
    spende time in reading bookes, that worthy Clarks have pend:

---

[31] Marginal Gloss: A sinne & a shame before the gods and men also.

[32] Marginal Gloss: Hark you worthe Matrons the counsel of mortal Helen.

In steede of Lutes and other harmonie,
    your willing eares a while to learning lende.

So *Cupid* and his Lore you shall forget,[33]
    with all such driftes as he and his doe drive:
Of slaunder and reproche you shall escape the net,
    and Fame with golden trumpe shal sound your vertue
Thus winning noble name, your lines shall end, line,
    so vertuouslye that after vitall breath,
The Gods theyr Aungels for your spirite shall sende,
    to dwell with them in blisse, thus Scripture sayth.

And with these wordes cast almost on the shore,
    the woefull wretch with toyled wearye bones,
With all the haste in flood doth laye the Ore,
    that headlong Boate and all, doth flee attonce.
Where hissing Serpentes swarme as thicke as haile,
    that likewise wayted in theyr subtile kinde
With whetted stinges this Lady to assaile,
    for to rewarde her lothsome lustfull minds.

And as wee did perceyve shee wisht that we,
    to every worthy wight report should make,
Howe fornicatours in Hell rewarded bee,
    and howe the Gods uppon them vengeaunce take.
For straight alas amid that ouglye lake,
    her hande shee putteth up, and bad farewell:
Thus endles paines her former talke gan slake,
    more newes of her, I am not able to tell.

For why, the hissing of the wicked wormes,
    with fome of surging lakes, that rores against the rocks
And furious thondering flames, that boiles and brommes,
    beside the fowles of many filthye flockes,

---

[33] Marginal Gloss: The vertuous and godlye Wives be shrinde among the Gods for ever.

On Helmettes, Billes, yeelde many mortall knockes,
    with thumping of the Cannons cruell shottes:
The noyse of Chaines, and wrenche of bandes and locks,
    with smorid smoke, of boyling Pitche in Pottes.

As fearefull daunse of Chimneys builded hye,[34]
    and fall of Turrets, that sleyeth man and childe:
With widowes, whose fatherles children doe crye,
    theyr plaintes alas, all Joye of hope exilde.
To heare them grone, whome mortall weapon spoilde,
    with crashe of staves, that then in peeces flowe:
A voyce cryed vengeaunce (on them that were defilde
    with spilling guiltlesse blood) that might not doe thereto.

Another voyce, went hurling up and downe,
    woe, woe, to such as strife sturre up or brewe:
And specially by warres, to sacke both Citie and Towne,[35]
    laye waste the soyle and ploughe, where Oxen drewe.
From mirthe to mourning, all to chaunge a newe,
    wives and children, spoilde before eache others face:
The causers ever, the first them selves that rewe,
    and woe still bee to you, that have so litle grace.

These soundes of sorrowes, that rose so many waies,
    berev'de us *Helen,* poore wretche in flaming Seas.

            * * * * *

The Bookes verdicte upon *Helen*

Who hearde me tell this tale, that doth their eyes witholde,
Or that their collours doth not pale, to heare it read or
   tolde?
Is any heart so harde, that woulde not melt to heere?
You Ladies doe you not regarde, the fall of bewties peere?

---

[34] Marginal Gloss: The Innocents blood fled wilfullye, craveth vengeance

[35] Marginal Gloss: A voyce.

And have you locked up, salt flooddes within your eyes?
Why have you kist *Medusas* cup? Your heartes why doe they frees?
Hath Lethea Lake bewicht all you that living be?
Nor hath not pittie never twicht your heartes to mourne with me?
Perhappes you doe disdaine to heare such tydings tolde:
But yet you may be glad againe, I saye both young and olde.
Ulisses wife doth loase no fame nor honour here:
No, No, nor any one of those, that live in godlie fere.
Nor yet the good *Alcestis*, doth catch no blotte nor staine:[36]
Nor *Griselda* doth not loase the least of *Hippos* happie gaine,
I am assured this, that *Cleopatra* winnes
Through Fame a triple blisse, loe now my tale beginnes.
For *Cresyde* she is one, whose face may blush to heare,
Of Helens life, that now is gon, ungracious *Circes* peere.
In bewtie *Venus* matche, *Arcynos* worse by mutche:
Medeas sleyghtes shee had to catch, whome pleased me to towche.

---

[36] Robinson's list of wicked and dangerous women and notoriously beautiful women to compare with Helen of Troy starts with Penelope ('Ulisses Wife') and ends with Niobe. Alcestis: was the daughter of Pelias and offers herself as a sacrifice for her husband Admetus (king of Thessalay) who forgot to make a sacrifice to Artemis on his wedding day. With the help of Apollo he receives permission from the Fates that someone may die in his place. His wife Alcestis offers herself and is saved by either Persephone or Heracles. Griselda is the topic of Chaucer's *The Clerk's Tale*, where the Clerk relates the story of Patient Griselda whose love is cruelly tested by her husband Lord Walter and she is found true. Hippos, short for Hippodamia whose suitors were required to challenge her father in a chariot race. Pelops, who was cut up and served at at banquet by his father Tantalus and later reassembled by the gods, won her hand, married her and they bore the infamous brothers Thyestes and Atreus. Cleopatra is, of course, the ancient ruler of Egypt and the most often cited Ptolemic ruler. She committed suicide when Octavian took Alexandria in 30 BCE. Venus is the Roman goddess of beauty. Circes (or Circe) is the powerful godess who guards islands in the East (according to Homer) and changed Odysseus' men into pigs; she was frequently cited as a wanton and a temptress, the pursuit of which turns men into beasts. Arcynos: I can find no other mention of this goddess. Medea, who also appears in Robinson's journey, was the daughter of Aeëtes and Eidyia; she became an example of a barbarian expert in scheming. Symons refers to a crafty person, as used in John Leslie's *Treatise of Treasons Against Queene Elizabeth* which appeared anonymously in 1572, (STC 23617.5), to describe the techniques William Cecil and Nicholas Bacon used against Catholics. Sylenos is the Greek god of wine-making. Niobe is the daughter ot Tantalus and Amphion and boasted that because she had more children than Leto she was better than the goddess. Leto sent her two children (Apollo and Artemis) to kill of of Niobe's children.

I say its such as these, that *Synons* shiftes doe use:
And vertuous studies seeme to lese, on wanton toyes to muse.
I meane such retchelesse dames, that play *Sylenos* part:
To winne such merry pleasaunt games, as teache sir Cupids art.
Loe these are they and such, that ought with shamefaste looke,
To be abasht when they shall touche, or vew this simple booke.
Sith Helens faultes are knowne, and yours in secret hyd:
Take heede least you be overthrowne, as Helen hath betide.
And blame hir vices all, but wofull chaunce bewayle:
For while I live even so I shall, if sorrow might prevaile.
And sith it was your happes, so worthy a Dame to have:
To warne you from such after claps, as turne you might to scath.
Whose face did staine the rest, of all that earthly were
Adornde in every joynt and drest, most like dame Bewties pere.
Therefore from sacred breast, what scalding sighes streight sende,
Let not your christall eyes have rest, to thinke of Helens ende.
With *Niob* bathe your face in teares, for Helens sake,
Unto the Gods call, cry, for grace, for to escape the lake,
Where Helen thus with paines, in riven boate doth rowe.
In fiery seas she still remaines, because shee was utrewe.

RICHARD ROBINSON

Newes betwene the *Pope* and *Pluto*, and of the Proclamation about the Ladder twixt Hell and Heaven

Thus leaving Helen[37] in endlesse woe and paine,
Through irkesome vale from crag to crag we crept:
Tormented sprites we hearde of eche side plaine,
Thousandes thousandes, schryking cryed and wept,
Linckt fast in chaynes, with cruell Keepers kept.
    Whose name and actes we listed not to crave,
    But passed foorth to vewe the monstrous cave.

Till at the length to a steepe and hawtie hill
We chaunst to come whereas me thought I see,
One rowling up a stone that tumbleth on him still.[38]
Thus night and daye from toyling rests not hee.
Also Duke *Theseus* for his tirannys,
    Bitten with Vipers and torne with Toades in sunder,
    In a pitte or puddle, that belched light and thunder.

Aeneas following *Sibil* rounde about that denne,
Up hill from crag to crooked *Torre* he runnes,
His wandering limmes still treades the filthie fenne,
In hope to have in sight that alwayes shunnes.
Also women drewe water in buckets that runnes.
    With very manye mo to long to name,
    As then me thought had plagues much like the same.

But as wee went mee thought I sawe a glade,[39]
That made a shoe as it a passage were,
Which was in deede of very purpose made,
From thence to Rome erectes a mightie stere[40]

---

[37] See the Note on the Text (p.12) for a discussion of this reference to Helen.

[38] Marginal Gloss: Sisiphus for his desolute and vicious living.

[39] Marginal Gloss:: There are moe wayes to Hell then one.

[40] Marginal Gloss: This is the waye from Rome to Pluto.

And *Gorgon* with a Clubbe was Porter there,
    Except from Rome, in, there he might not passe,
    Or else some suche as trusted in the Masse.

This way passe soules from paines to endelesse blisse,[41]
When please the Pope to sende his letters thither,
Morpheus and I experience saw of this,
The Popes man and wee met altogither,
Who brought Pardons packt up in a bouget of lether.
    Besides letters that to *Pluto* then he delivered,
    On the which *Pluto* looked, perusde, and considered.

Whereupon *Pluto* his counsell calde straight,
A filthie heape of crooked noble states,
To here their mindes because it was of weight,
To gratifie the Pope and all his holye mates,
Sende for the messenger, and so these wordes debates.
    My friende (quoth hee) tha'rt welcome to this place,
    So are they all that love thy maysters grace.

But by the floodes of dreadfull flaming *Styx*,
The newes thy maister writtes doe grieve my guttes ful sore,
For revenge, these clawes as sharpe as thornie prickes,
Shall tosse and teare the sprites of many a score,
(Ah worthy Pope) thy decay I much deplore·
    A Cater for my Kitchine, provider of the praye,
    What mervell though I curse the cause of thy decaye?

And with these wordes his scowling face lets poure,
The gushing floodes and spowtes of fier red,
He gnasht his teeth and gan to glowte full soure,
With belching breath, to the messenger thus sayde:
Take here an aunswere unto my supreme heade.
    (Byd him be merye) I shall assistaunce sende,
    To taxe all suche, as with him doe contende.

---

[41] Marginal Gloss: The waye that soules passe thorowe betwene heaven and hel.

With a Romishe thankes, the messenger packeth,
Charged with the letters that *Pluto* doth sende,
Poste horses by commission in eache place he taketh,
Untill he arived at the stayers ende,
Whereas from *Lymbo* to Roome he should ascende,
    Being a lustie Lurdaine a Fryer of Saint Fraunces,
    Twixt Rome and hel from steppe to steppe he daunces.

Thus the Fryer fled we hearde no more of him,
But straight on a stage a Trumpet sounded was,
Whereunto assembled such soules as for sinne,
Were sent by the Pope to be punisht alas,
Who thought to be pardoned by vertue of the masse.
    Else hoping to heare of the Popes comming thither,
    Then thinking to be releast from thence altogither.

When silence was made with much a doe,
This ill faste Herraulde these wordes then declared:
That many men to the Pope were untrue,
And their large offrings and devotions nowe spared,
For to come to God other meanes they prepared.
    Having no trust in the Pope nor his traditions,
    But cal him the Captaine of Idolatrous superstitions.

To our Prince *Pluto* his letters doe declare,
That toward the North Pole Gods word is so embraste:
That no man for pardons will give mony nor ware,
(In Englande especially) he is utterly disgraste·
Except among a fewe here and there that are plaste.
    That with their friendes in nowkes and odde holes,
    Sing a masse of *Requiem* for al christian soules.

Which is to no purpose the money being gone,
That maintayned his grace and all his whole rowte,
His Cardinals, his Abbottes, his Friers, with sir John,

His Nunnes, and his Ancrees[42], and all be thrust out,
His Pardnors go begging and wandring about.
    The shavelings be shronken that once bare the swaye,
    Their credite and customes be runne to decaye.

And *Boner* that bolstred the beames of his glorie,
Lyeth Sunke in the sandes that onse beare the blade:
That many a Christian therewith made full sorie,
A while in Christes Vineyarde he cut a great glade,
And stoute *Storie* that all the sturre made.[43]
    Gardiner is wanting that was the blood letter,
    And *Fecknam* is fast that was the clocke setter.[44]

Besyde an infinite number within that same Ile,
That now be decayed and worne out of minde:
Banisht is *Babilon* that florisht ere awhile,

---

[42] [f. ancre, Anchor - n.2, with Fr. fem. ending -esse, -ess; cf. anchresse in Palsgr. 1530. In ME. ancre was used for both sexes. A rarer fem was Anchoritess - A female anchorite, a nun. *OED*.

[43] Marginal Gloss: Storie·Gardiner. Fecknam.

[44] John Story (1503/4? – 571). According to John Foxe, Story was 'by hys co[n]fession, the chefest cause and doer, in pursuyng most of the martyrs to death'; 'In su[m]ma: Story worsse then Boner' (BL, Lansdowne MS 109, fol. 52r). In May 1560 Story was taken to the Fleet prison, along with Bonner and John Feckenham – he escaped two years later but was captured in 1570 and sentenced to death in 1571 for treason. Julian Lock, ('John Story', *DNB*). Stephen Gardiner (c.1495-1555) was a theologian who studied with Erasmus and who became indispensable to Cardinal Wolsey and Henry VIII, and, later, one of the most influential Catholic polemicists, for which he was imprisoned during Edward's short reign. During the reign of Mary Tudor Gardiner was freed and became one of the pioneers for the restoration of Catholicism in England. He strongly advocated the arrest and imprisonment of Elizabeth and proposed that Mary declare her a bastard. John Foxe claimed that he even ordered Elizabeth's execution in the Tower, but there is no conclusive evidence for this. He died a natural death before the end of Mary's reign ('Gardiner', *DNB*). John Feckenham (c. 1510-1584) was Queen Mary's chaplain and confessor. He attended the disputations with Thomas Cramner, Hugh Latimer and Nicholas Ridley. He was sent by Mary to question Lady Jane Grey (then Lady Guildford Dudley) about her treason and Protestantism and later stood by her as she awaited her death on the scaffold. He also questioned Princess Elizabeth but when she was crowned in 1559, Feckenham was allowed to remain at Westminster Abbey despite remaining true to the Catholic faith: 'As the last de facto – as opposed to titular – abbot he has a prescriptive place in Catholic and especially Benedictine history; he belongs in equal measure to the old English monasticism of his first profession, and to resurgent tradition which reckons its descent from Marian Westminster' ('Feckenham', *DNB*).

And the way to *Jerusalem* by the Gospell they finde
The Pope they repute to be a guide blinde.
    They passe not a pin, for his blessinges nor curses,
    Let him saye what he will, they holde fast their purses.

And in place of his friendes are starte up his foes,
And one cruell Captaine that workes all the griefe,
A *Jewell* of Christ Jesus gave *Harding* the bloes,[45]
Confuting his fables in spite of his teeth,
Hee feedes the poore flocke with Christian beleefe.
    Squencht is the confidence I say of our Harding,
    Thers none young nor olde that esteemes him a farthing.

One *Barthlet*[46] wee may ban throughout this whole vale:
And so may the Pope with Candle, Booke and Bell,
In the Papall pedigrewe, hee tels such a tale,
That all Romish Roges may rore to heare tell,
That Christians had knowledge of the trumprye they sell.
    For he tippes up the sacke, and all poureth out,
    From the first to the last, he rappes the whole route.
(This and much more) being the just cause,
Of the Popes great plague and miserable want:
(I meane of money) to maintaine his lawes,

---

[45] Marginal Gloss: Juell. Harding. Robinson here refers to the theologian Thomas Harding (1516-1572) and John Jewel. Harding dallied with Protestantism but then confirmed his strong Catholic stance with Mary's accession. In 1555 he became confessor to Stephen Gardiner, bishop of Winchester, who appointed him as one of the executors of his will. On Elizabeth's accession Harding stood by his beliefs and his movements were limited by the ecclesiastical commissioners but he moved to France where he was eventually appointed to a professorship at Douai. While in France he began a correspondence with John Jewel, whom he had met at Oxford: 'The so-called 'Jewel–Harding controversy' arose from the 'challenge sermon' which Jewel, bishop of Salisbury, delivered at Paul's Cross in 1559, and from Jewel's *Apologia Ecclesiae Anglicanae* of 1562' ('Thomas Harding', *DNB*). While at Oxford John Jewell (1522-1571) met and befriended the Italian theologian turned reformer, Pietro Martire Vermigli, known in England as Peter Martyr. Jewel fled to the continent during Mary's reign and returned shortly after her death when he was appointed Bishop of Salisbury ('John Jewel', *DNB*).

[46] Possibly a small 'barth' or sheltered space for livestock, *OED* says: 1573 Tusser Husb. (1878) 73 Warme barth give lams. Ibid. 62 In tempest.Warme barth, under hedge, is a sucker to beast.

Perforce must perswade you, that here make your plaint,
Considering Gods worde hath him on the tainte.
    You wofull soules that in Purgatorie lye,
    Must yet here remaine there is good cause why.

(Which is this) you know the Pope hath been at cost,
To found betwixt *Pluto* and *Rome* these stayres:
And nowe it is like, that his labour is lost,
Because that his customes and credite thus weares:
Yet hee hath set Priests, Munkes, Nunnes, and Friers.
    And the rest of his Rable in hande for to make,
    A Ladder to reache into Heaven for your sake.

And up it was reared· yeares long a goe,[47]
And well underset with Dyrges and Masses:
With Popishe Props, thousandes on a roe,
As Pardons, Buls, Idols, Holy water, and Ashes:
Palmes, and holy Bread, and many olde Trashes,
    Lampes, Lightes, Crossing and Creeping,
    And all to redresse your pitifull weeping.

Singing, and Ringing, with Belles every where,
Sensing, and Fensing with Booke Bell and Candle:
Cursing, and Praying, of Muncke, Nun, and Frier,
Night, daye and hower, al thing for to handle:
Like workemen worthy, not bunglers to Scamble.
    A building to bolte so hye in the skyes,
    doth crave Cunning workemen, and such as are wise.

But loe (alas) the Popes willing minde,[48]
For money to release you of these bitter paines:
So many thousandes strove this Ladder to climbe,
That you mist the Heaven, and hee his great gaines:
For bending it brake, with waight of your Chaines.

---

[47] Marginal Gloss: The building of the Lader and the timber with the workmen.

[48] Marginal Gloss: The cause of the fall thereof.

By meanes whereof, therein, who put trust,
World without ende, remaine heere they must.
And too short it was, by full ten degrees,[49]
And never could reach Gods glorye and blisse:
Although hee, and his, were as busie as Bees,
In thende it woulde haue provided but this:
Wherefore bee contented no remeedye is,
    Tyl the Ladder bee mended, hence to dispatche yee,
    Or else that the Pope, come him selfe for to fetch yee.

The Gospell of Christ, hath throughly confounded,
Not onely this Ladder, of the Popes owne device:
But also destroyde al them that first founded
The painted Helles, and paper Paradice:
Heare among us, they shall playe theyr Price.
    Theyr stinking Idolatrye, and vile Superstition,
    As holye as they bee, heare findes no remission.

Therefore it is *Pultos* pleasure that you knowe,
What fortune hath hapned, your Father the Pope:
Hee him selfe to Heaven, is not able to goe,
Except Saint *Peter,* hale him up in a Roape:
Or that hee chaunse to bee pulde by his Coape,
    By our Lady of Walsingham, & sweet Roode of Chester,[50]
    Else his porcion in Heaven, is scant worth a Testar.

These wordes being saide, hee dismounteth the stage,
Saying, vengeance, and torment, protect *Plutos* grace:
At the which cryed out with terrible rage,
Both yong and olde that were in that place:
A sight to sorrowfull, in beholding theyr case.

---

[49] Marginal Gloss: The tormented soules perswaded to dwell for ever in paines.

[50] The *Lady of Walsingham* and the *Rood of Chester* are both Catholic shrines in England dating from the Medieval period.

(I meane) of al such, as put trust in the Masse,
These Newes made theyr torments much worse then it
was.

To see the sorrowfull sort hale one another,
Crying out on the Popes, and his shavelinges there:
The Father, the Sonne, the Daughter, the Mother,
The Uncle, the Aunte, and Grandsier appeare:
To the ninthe degree, thousandes there were
    Both Ritch and Poore, that trusted to the Masse,
    Not one of them all, but I am sure there hee was.

Some cryde fye of Idols, and some of holye water,
Some of Supersticion, and some of *Scala celi*[51]
Other some lamented, the mumbling of Lady Psalter,
(Alas) quod another, this will not prevaile yee,
Now maye you see, their trumprye doth faile yee.
    So it doth them selves, for loe where they lye,
    That late hoyst theyr Gods, in Haulters full hye.

And loe (quoth hee) where they hee singing a Masse,
Pope *Alexander,* Pope *Jhoan,* and both under a stoale:
See you not the sweete blood of hayles in a glasse,
Which Idoll brought hither many a poore soule?
A Pardoner mee thinke standes by with a scrowle.
    Some officer bee like of Saint Johns sweete Frary,
    Looke who is in his bookes it is best you prepare yee.

---

[51] The ladder to the skies ('Scala coeli') refers to the 'sacred steps' in Rome that Catholics believe are the same steps Christ climbed when he received judgment from Pilate. The steps, like the cave of Saint Patrick's Purgatory in Ireland, have been used as a place for earthly penance where Christians pray for salvation in the direction of Heaven. But the steps became just another feature of Indulgences Catholics could purchase from the Church for their salvation. Avale's juxtaposition of Bonner's rejection of 'justification' and belief in the ladder to heaven is satirised in Bonner's repeated laments that he is not in purgatory now, but in Hell. Robinson makes more of the relationship between Bonner and Hell by imagining him as one of Pluto's most honoured subjects. Cf. Lemeke Avale's invective against Bonner, *A commemoration or dirige of bastarde Edmonde Boner* (1569). Avale's Bonner discusses his 'Romish waies' and says that he could not bear the Protestant idea of justification by faith alone. 'Justification I could not abide, / Specially if it came on Christes side: / I will clime heavens walles with *Scala coeli* (Ab2r).

At which wordes such a number brake out,
Of Caves and Sinkes on every side:
As Tipling Bibs, and Suckers of growte,
Sect Sowers, and Brewbates, thyther fast bide:
Tutors, and Teltales, in euery nowke cryde.
    Pickethankes and Prowlers, beare holy water,
    Their maisters (being worldlings) sayd *Confiteor,* and *Misereator.*

Flattery light Lampes, to our Lady of grace,
Hipocrisie, calde them up to the offering,
Saint *Anne* of Buckstones[52] was washing a pace:
But *Lucre* was lifting small pence to the Coffering.
At shrieft they were close in every place.
    Two faces in one hoode, the Crosse then did beare,
    Whereat abhomination, beganne for to sweare.

Great devision there seemed to bee,
All that were there· did knocke on theyr breast:
But (alas) to late for to crye then *Peccavi,*[53]
Althoughe the Pope both Crossed and bleste,
For when hee lookte backe, at *Ite missa est:*[54]
When *Dan* Limlifter, the Candles should oute,

---

[52] St. Anne's well in Buxton, a place of pilgrimage for Catholics.

[53] Latin: I have sinned.

[54] 'Ite missa est' is traditionally said at the end of a Roman Catholic mass. *The New Advent Encyclopaedia* entry reads: 'This is the versicle chanted in the Roman Rite by the deacon at the end of Mass, after the Post-Communions. It is our formula of the old dismissal (apolysis) still contained in all liturgies. It is undoubtedly one of the most ancient Roman formulæ, as may be seen from its archaic and difficult form. [. . .] The medieval commentators were much exercised to explain the meaning of the strange expression. Durandus (Rationale, IV, 57) suggests several interpretations. It has been thought that a word is omitted: Ite, missa est finita; or est is taken absolutely, as meaning 'exists', is now an accomplished fact'. The real explanation seems to lie rather in interpreting correctly the word missa. Before it became the technical name of the holy Liturgy in the Roman Rite, it meant simply 'dismissal'. [. . .] [it] was always answered by the obvious response Deo gratias, implying thanks that the Sacrifice has been offered -- is now complete. [. . .] In the First Roman Ordo, immediately after it the text continues "Then the seven candlesticks are carried before the pontiff . . . to the sacristy"' http://www.newadvent.org/cathen/08253a.htm [Date accessed: 1/12/2008].

All flewe on a fire their Colledge through out.
   Howe the Ladder was amended, that lately was craishte,
   After that time trulie of no man I aihste.

The rewarde of *Medea* for hir wicked actes, and false deceyving of hir father, sleying of hir children and hir owne Brother, and working by inchauntment. This historie is merveylous tragicall, and a good example for Women[55]

O Dreadfull *Stix,* boyle up thy poysoned floodes,
    and cruell *Cacus* torments newe devise:
Give sentence *Mynos* of theyr guiltlesse bloodes
    that murderers handes have shed in any wise.
You furies fell, why doe you yet despise
    with greater plagues my paines for to increase,
And for to see the bloode of Innocents arise,
    whose mouthes from crying vengance never cease?

And where shee stoode, hir heade shee cast awry,
    In wofull plight as ever wretch might be,
And so by chaunce at length did *Morpheus* spie,
    whose open jawes, gryed streight to him and me.
Saying *Morpheus* come and bring thy frinde with thee,
    a greater newes to learne thou shalt in hast·
Of all thou hast perused with thine eye,
    I worthy am the greatest griefe to taste.

I knowe thou camst from place where *Helen* rowes,
    in th'irkesome lake where doubtfull Dragons bee,
And yet hir wicked life and mine God knowes
    are not to be comparde, although that shee,
For certaine yeares lived in adulterie,
    and betrayed hir husbande, good noble *Menelaus,*

---

[55] Robinson's account of Medea focuses on her as a murderess and deceiver. The story of how Medea's love for Jason, her assistance in his quest for the Golden Fleece and the later murder of Jason's lover Creusa and her own children (by Jason) after Jason abandoned her, could be found in at least three existing sources which Robinson may have accessed: Studley's translation of Seneca's tragedy *Medea* (1566); Arthur Golding's translation of Ovid's *Metamorphoses* (1567); and John Lydgate's *Fall of Princes*, which maintains the emphasis on Medea as a victim to her own unbridled desire for revenge. Robinson omits the Senecan emphasis on the gradual process by which Medea's grief turns to madness (*furor*) and leads to her murderous actions.

Set *Greece* and *Troy* at great mortalitie,
    shed bloode, sackt Cities, banisht godly lawes.

(Yet this hir fact, not halfe like mine alas)
    why doth not Hell brayde out hir stinking breth?
And my desertes much worse then *Helens* was,
    (Hell spew thy spight) devoure me once with death.
Will neyther ruthe, nor spight, stirre up your heartes?
    will none of those once moove you to dispatche,
But will you alwayes playe such cruell partes?
    more wishing death, more lingering life I catche.

(Quoth *Morpheus*) what is thy name declare it,
    where wast thou borne, why art thou plagued tell?
(Quoth shee) againe, no more I will not spare it,
    Make hast (quoth hee) I may not tarry well.
A'the which, with greevous scriking yell,
    shee did describe hir wicked crimes and name,
I am (quoth shee) so punisht here in Hell,
    that passeth wight with tongue to tell the same.

My name is *Medea* (quoth shee) most trewe,
    daughter I was to *Oetes* that worthy king:
Which had the Ramme where fleece of golde ygrewe,
    the greatest jewell of any earthly thing.
Which was my fathers, and in his keeping,
    watcht with a Bull, that was of worthy might,
And a Dragon with mightie poysoned sting,
    that stoutly kept this Ramme both day and night.

Many a worthy Prince and champion stoute,
    had lost their lives in venture giving,
Which never brought their purpose yet about,
    nor no man to this day but *Jason* living.
Devoured they were by the ravening of these two,

he lost his life, that thought to win his shooes:⁵⁶
These beastes so violently did all men pursue,
   that for to die might neyther will nor choose.

Whiche was my Fathers chiefe of exaltacion,
   hee florished in wealth no Prince his like:
Drad hee was of everye lande and Nation,
   hee forste no strength of all his foes a mite.
And yet of treasure all, he sette his chiefe delite
   on mee his Daughter deare, that sought his griefe:
I quite my Fathers love with mortall spite,
   I playde the whore, the murdresse and the theefe.

Harke nowe *Morpheus,* what a parte I playde,
   by my Father deare my Brother and my Childe:⁵⁷
And what a noble quene I afterward betrayed,
   with many more by wicked arte I broilde.
And other some I banishte and exilde,
   by Devillishe wayes as women shoulde not doe:
For why they ought with mercye to bee milde,
   and not theyr wicked willes for to pursue.

Beholde howe I did nature quite forsake,
   for this I did as true as here I am:
When *Jason* came this conquest for to make,
   (false traitour I) through mee the fleece hee wanne·
For arte of wicked Charme I straight beganne,
   for *Jason* sake my Parent to betraye:
Dismaide my Father sillye Aged man,
   abandoned his house, with *Jason* ranne awaye.
By incantacion: I brought it so to passe,

---

⁵⁶ Marginal Gloss: An olde saying: all covet all love.

⁵⁷ Medea's father was Aeëtes, King of Colchain Aia, which Apollonius of Rhodes says, 'lies pressed against the very edge of Pontos and of the earth' (*Jason and the Golden Fleece,* trans. Richard Hunter. Oxford University Press, Oxford: 1998 Bk II, line 420). Medea's brother was Apsyrtus.

that *Jason* slewe bothe Bull and griesly Beast:
Atchiev'de all thinges as his desire was,
    for of my Brother I caused him possest,
That in the Regall seate, should crowne & scepter beare
    in *Colcos* Lande it booted not to rest:
For why my Father so greate an hoast did reare.
    with fleese to flye, we thought it was the best.

For why harde by my Father followed fast,
    But to escape his handes, harke what I did:
I kilde my Brother, his armes and legges I cast
    Throughout the fielde whereas my Father rid·
Which when my Father sawe, so ill betide,
    and knewe his sonne thus martyrred for to bee:
With woefull cheare to get them uppe straight hide·
    togeather (alas) eache chopped peece layde hee.

Then downe his Aged face, doeth tumble teares apace·
    and up in armes the Martyred head doeth gette:
Oh Sonne most deare, alas (quod hee) for grace,
    and many a kisse on deadlye mouth doth sette.
And then with nayles, his face he rentes and teares,
    that downe the purple streames of blood doe flee:
And readye death within his face appeares,
    but styll he cryed, (alas) deare sonne for thee.

To tell but halfe the morning that hee made,
    no doubte your eyes like conduit spoutes would run,
For verye woe hee pulleth out a blade,
    to slea him selfe for sorrowe of his sonne.
But yet his men and servauntes chaunste to come,
    my carefull Father there they did prevent:
Or else no doubte more mischiefe had beene done·
    and all through mee, accurst and disobedient.

Then after stormes of many woefull plaintes,
    perswaded by suche men as wittye were:
Like as *Apelles Agamemnon*[58], paintes,
    I maye compare my Fathers dreirye cheere:
Then in meane while, that hee was stayed there,
    with speede from *Colchas Jason,* and I did passe
For my Brothers funerall, hee builded Aulters fayre
    to Sacrifice upon, as then the maner was.

Loe by my Father thus I playde the theefe,
    'gainst nature and womanhood my Brother slewe·
And used witchcraft against the true beleefe,
    and like a Traitres, awaye with *Jason* flewe.
Haste thou ever hearde of any so untrue?
    To playe like part I thincke did never none:
Naye *Morpheus* yet more mischiefe did I brewe,
    for after this I murdered many a one.

Through *Nigromancie, Jason* being olde,
    from crabbed crooked Age, I made him yong againe:
Livelye and lightsome, active and bolde,
    and purelye purged in everye pulse and vain.
And Trees being dead I made beare fruite againe,
    which increased my credite, more then ever it was:
Through false crafte, I causde *Pelleus* be slaine,
    by his Daughters handes I brought it so passe.

Whome I made beleeve, as *Jason* did.
    that *Pelleus*[59] theyr Father should youth achieve:
And tolde them playne in doing as I bid,

---

[58] Appeles, 'painter of Colophon, later of Ephesus (sometimes called Coan because of the Coan 'Aphrodite'). He is mentioned more frequently and generally considered better than any other painter' OCD.

[59] Pelias, son of Tyro and Poseidon and father of Alcestis. He devised the challenge of the Golden Fleece to get rid of Jason, who had rightful claims to his throne in Ioclus. In Hesiod he is punished for not worshipping Hera who allows Jason and Medea to convince Pelias's daughters to cut him up under the guise that when Medea boils his body parts he will be rejuvenated, OCD.

hee should bee altered newe, not feeling paine nor grefe.
Thus I illuding them, they thought it true,
    (So did *Pelleus* him selfe) that time good man:
That being slaine from age to youth a newe,
    hee shoulde bee chaunged by killing of a Ram.

(The trueth was nothing soe) it was my fetche,
    to cause his Daughters, their Fathers blood to shed:
An olde Ram I badde them slea and wittely to watche,
    that no man sawe, when they to worke procede.
But (quod I) looke that your Father bleede
    in one vessell, and with this Ram at once:
And doing thus, I sayde that by and by with speede,
    theyr Father should arise with youthful flesh and bones.

These sillye Sisters and Daughters to this man,
    beleeved well this subtile tale of mine·
And as I bad, they slewe an aged Ram,
    and so they did theyr Father deare in fine.
Beleeving faithfullye by power devine,
    that theyr olde Father should bee made yong:
(Alas) which was not so, but onelye crafte of mine,
    to make an ende of him whome I had hated long.

Thus exited I, by crafte theyr worke alas,
    and dead lyeth theyr father bleeding fast.
But harke, *Morpheus* harke, how it then came to passe,
    mischiefe hath ever her due rewarde at last.
I thought this wicked deede, that thus was done and past,
    woulde best have pleased *Jason,* then my Lorde:
Which chaunste not so, for hee with all the hast
    fled from mee quite, and all my actes abhorde.

And so to *Corinthe,* to *Creon,* then the King
    hee tooke his waye as straight as thing might bee:
Who had a Daughter called *Crusa,* (bewties darling)
    whome Jason married, and so refused mee,

Whereat Dame Fame sound up her Trumpet hye,
    eache living eare was filled with the same:
Which made mee broyle as whot, as gleyde might bee,
    till I had spilde this tender noble Dame.

Which through *Magike,* and vile Conjuration,
    A cofer I invented with divers Jewels more:
Subtillye contrived of a straunge fashion,
    with the which to *Creuso,* I made my sonnes to goe,
To present the same, that livelye Ladye toe,
    who gratefullye receyved it, but yet (alas) beguilde:
For through my arte, when as it was undoe,
    there flewe foorth fire, that burnde both man and child.

Consumde to dust this Ladye fresh and gaye,
    burnde all the pallace five yardes within the grounde:
Urged *Jason* him selfe to flee away,
    or else with fire he had beene streight confound.
Many a wofull heart I made within that stounde,
    the Clowdes themselves, bewayling teares let fall.
The rockes and hilles brake out their plainting sounde,
    beside the guiltlesse bloode, that did for vengance call.

Of noble *Jason* thus the heart I slewe,
    who thought to be revengde of mine iniquitie:
Towards me when I perceyv'de he drew,
    my two sonnes left alive, without compassion or pitie,
Which were both tender, well made, and wittie,
    of my body begot, and naturallye borne,
For malice to their father *Jason,* amyd the Citie,
    I cut their throtes (and made their bodies torne,

With wilde horses) up and downe the streete,
    beside much mischiefe more than this be sure.
In all this stincking vale, yet did thou never meete
    with any wretch that did like greefe procure.
But who so ever meanes, in wickednesse to byde,
    or leade a Tyrauntes life, in the end shall have rewarde,

According his deserts, this cannot be denyed,
  Though mortall fleshe thereto have no regarde.
And then (quod she) thou knowest my name and why
  that I am thus tormented in *Stygion* pitte,
O that witches and Conjurers knew so well as I,
  of Joves mightie doome that doth in heaven sitte,
Then woulde they mende, if they had grace or witte,
  To serve the Lorde woulde set theyr whole delight:
And disobedient children woulde their follye flitte,
  assuredly the Lorde at length doth smite.

And with these wordes her paines increaste so sore,
  (But that shee sayde) report good *Morpheus* thus:
Or else at all wee heard her saye no more,
  but that shee shrikte as one that tormented is.
Thus seeing the reward of her wicked deedes,
  Wee stayed a while her tormentes to behold:
Which at a moment, both daye and hower breedes,
  much more then can by any tongue bee tolde.

To see the staring Devilles with fiery speares,
  on Dragons backes with poisoned pimples pight:[60]
As at a Quintan, at *Medea,* eche Tyrant beares,
  and through her runnes, that trickling blood appeares.
Then from the scalding heart, by violence out teares,
  Hote flames of fire, at woundes on every side,
Monsters with hornes, and lothsome louped eares,
  Ranne on this wretch, with gnashing teeth they cryed.

The blood by murder, this wicked wretche had shed,
  thondered vengeaunce, whose terrible noyse,
Heapte double paines upon her wretched head,
  and filde that dreadeful vale, (alas) with woeful noise.
Innumerable of Witches, out of theyr Cabbins rose,
  with screming scrikes, they yelded lovde and hye.

---

[60] Marginal Gloss: The torments of Stigion.

Hote Pitche and Brimstone, eache one on other throse,
   A Hell it selfe, mee thought it was to see.

Eache one in hande, begrypte a Butchers knife,
   the blades in fleshe on everye side they hide:
The throate, the Guttes, or nexte to ridde the life,
   the mortall woundes they make on every side.
Then straight with thundring throate *Maegaera* cryde,
   come, *Cacus,* come, bring double paine and woe:
Let wickednesse in endles flames bee fride,
   come, come, the Gods have sixte it soe

At which came *Cacus,* and Cloudes of fire shakes,
   more fearefull farre then blaste of storming winde
Eache pitte boylde up, the craggye mountayne quakes,
   all crawling creepes, the Snakes of Serpentes kinde.
No greater griefe, no damned spryte coulde finde,
   For out of flashe, to gleydes of glowing coale,
From paine, to paine, from place to place assignde,
   and al to toyle and teare the woefull soule.

And thus wee lefte this late rewarded Dame,
   and so adrest ourselves, to crooked *Charons* bote,
Where many a wandering spirite, had passage by the same,
   through boyling broath, three times as sulfer hote,
With muche a doe, at length wee passage gote,
   and downe the smoaking banckes, wee crepte on knee,
Tyll at the length by chaunce it was our lotte,
   twoo men to see tormented woefullye.

* * * * *

The Bookes verdicte upon *Medea*

Her cause who can bewaile, that plaide this butchers parte:
As from her father deare to steale, that lov'de her in his hart,

Her brother thus to slea, the Parentes hearts to kill:
And with a straunger ronne awaye, to feede her fleshly will.

The guiltlesse blood to sucke, of *Creuso worthy Dame:*
And all at once uppon a rocke, to wast in fiery flame.
Beside, her Children deare hath wounde with mortall knife.
The smiling Babes her body beare, bereft their tender life.
What eyes can stint from fluddes, whose eares doe understande
To cal to minde the gyltles bloods, shed by this womans handes:
What harme by witchraft done, it passeth tongue to tell:
Or any heart to thinke the somme, or hand to penne it well.
(Alas) whoe would have thought, that in a womans breast:
Dame nature would have let been wrought, to breede so much unrest:
But harde it is to trust, what ever that shee bee:
That to hir father is unjust, shee meanes the same to thee.
But loe you cruell Dames, that love your wils so much:
I speake it now to all your shames, if there be any such.
Medea now is gone, that all the bate did brewe:
Take heede among you there be none, with hir to proove untrewe.
You witches all take heede, you see how God rewardes:
And what appoynted is your meede, that divelish actes regardes.
Leave of your invocation, your crossings and your charmes:
(Alas) it is abomination, and doth increase your harmes.
You parents it is time, to looke your younglings to:
Least with this Prince, you say in fine, heartes case and child adue.
Keepe in your daughters strayght, best counsell I can geve:
Least that perhaps shee catch a bayte, that both your harts may greve.
And bring them up in feare, and godlie bookes to reede:
And then be sure that thou shalt heare, that wel thy chide shall speede
And banish wilie will, from out thy daughters place:
His sleyghtie shiftes will thousands spill, you know he wanteth grace
Let bouldenesse banisht be, lay libertie aside:
And looke you never doe agree, to paint them up in pride.

And so you shall rejoyce, your daughters dayes to see:
With *Helchias*[61] lift up your voyce, with prayse as glad as hee.
Thus farwell Virgins all, God guide you in his way:
I doubt not but *Medeas* fill, your tender heartes shall fraye.
And sith shee broyles in Hell, whereas release is none:
There I am sure that shee shall dwell, it helpeth not to mone.
I cannot weepe therefore, to thinke what partes shee playde:
Shee lost hir soule for evermore, hir name is quite decayde.
Take heede, hir gaines you see, the Gods not one doe spare:
For this or that, looke what they be, rewarded well they are.

---

[61] In the Apocrypha (2 Esdras 1:1) it says, 'the prophet Esdras, the son of Saraias, the son of Azarias, the son of Helchias, the son of Sadamias, the so[n] of Sadoc, the son of Achitob'. In Robert Greene's *The Mirror of Modesty*, he ascribes this name to Susanna's father – a story also inherited from the Apocrypha. That Robinson is thinking of this story is clear from his naming Helchias in a warning to parents about the dangers associated with beautiful daughters. Greene writes: 'This Joachim, willing to take a wife and to link himself in the holy league of matrimony, coveted carefully to find out such a match that he might neither have cause to rue his change nor repent of him his choice, knowing that after that know was once knit, had-I-wist would come too late. He therefore sought out one Susanna, the daughter of Helchias, a man who carefully sought to keep the law and took surpassing pains in the diligent instructing of his daughter, knowing that her virtuous qualities would be a comfort to him and a credit to herself' (Robert Greene, *The Mirror of Modesty*, London(1584) p.4). http://www.oxford-shakespeare.com/new_files_jan_07/Mirror%20of%20Modesty%20(1584).pdf [Date accessed: 27/11/08].

***Pope Alexander* the sixt rewarded for his wickednesse and odible lyfe, with his colledge of Cardinals, Bishops, Abbots, Moonckes, Freers, and Nunnes, with the rabble of greasie Priestes, and other members of Idolatry and superstition. &c**[62]

O Hell, O Hell, deserved long agoe,
    and raging Furies that beare immortall spight,
What doe you meane, why spare you any woe,
    that should increase our paine, & pleasure our delight?
Where is your woonted wrath, accustomed to thro
    among the soules unto your charge committed:
Come doe your worst, consume us all aro,
    dispatche us streight, lets be no longer Ditted.[63]

Thou filthy floode of Lymbos lurcking lake,
    From choaked pitte, come belche abroade thy flames:
Why come you not you Furies for to take
    a greater vengaunce, I call you by your names.
Spew out Plegethon, thy furious fiery flake,
    O Hell why vomitst not thy greatest gorge of all:
Once give consent a finall ende to make
    of us, that doe your wrath so gladly call.

---

[62] Pope Alexander the Sixth (b. 1431, pope 1492-1503) began his career as pope by executing justice and establishing order. He soon, however, started offering high positions and profitable marriages to his children and family members which then fuelled a conflict with Ferdinand I, King of Naples and later also with Charles VIII of France. In order to raise funds for his military operations he disposed of civil and spiritual privileges and offices ruthlessly. His reputation as a wicked and corrupt pope has been partly exaggerated and is not necessarily confirmed by historical evidence. After his deceased body was placed on the altar (next to burning candles) his face reportedly turned black and his nose, tongue and lips swelled up. Johann Burchard was a Papal Master of Ceremonies in the late fifteenth and early sixteenth centuries and recorded his perception of what happened to the pope's body after his death. In the following centuries accounts of Alexander's bad reputation continued – see for instance, Alexander Gordon's *The lives of Pope Alexander VI. and his son Cæsar Borgia: comprehending the wars in the reigns of Charles VIII. and Lewis XII. kings of France: and the chief transactions and revolutions in Italy, from the year 1492 to the year 1506.* (London, 1729).

[63] The MS is very unclear here. I have put 'Ditted' because it seems like the closest match. *OED* 'dit', def. 2: To stop or obstruct the course or way of.

Come ougly shapes from olde sepulchers sent,
   come filthy Fowles from loathsome boyling puddle,
Come monsterous Grypes, that *Tyrius* guttes hath rent,
   some Judge of Sprits, come, come increase our trouble.
Come Prince of darcknesse, give thy fearefull judgement,
   O Hell unfolde thy gates, and let the flaming steame
Make hast to increase our punishment,
    Dispatche us once, out of this endelesse trouble.

O vile Idolatrie, the Prince of perdicion,
   the waye thou directes to everlasting paines:
O filthie moment, and wicked superstition,
   O blynde doctrine, Interpretor of dreames.
O rotten relics with all your addicion,
   fye upon you all, sith thus it comes to passe.
Falsehoode in the end hath no remission,
   as witnesse our devillishe detestable mase.

And with these woordes, he caste his head a wrye,
   amonge the shaveling greasie chuffhead Friers:[64]
And seeing Morpheus standing present bye,
   the sawsie sorte of Priestes with Moonks and Nunnes appeares
At which this Pope beganne to roare and crye,
   alas (quod hee) beholde where Morpheus standes:
Hee will proclayme abroade that heare wee lye,
   that rule of Hell, and heaven did take uppo'ns.
What shall wee doe (quod hee) best call him hether,
   it hayneth so there is none other shifte:
Lets say wee come for Soules, they answered altogether,

---

[64] Pig-headed. CF. In *Actes and Momuments* (1563), Foxe recounts the martyrdom of Elizabeth Driver: 'The examination of Drivers wife before Doctor Spencer, the Chauncellor of Norwich'- and the questions asked of Mrs Driver by the chancellor and, 'a great chuffe-headed priest, that stode by, spake and asked her why she made not the Chauncellor an answer', page 1683, The John Foxe Project: http://www.hrionline. ac.uk/johnfoxe/main/12_1563_1683.jsp [Date accessed 17, July 2008].

and that wee meane to make a general shrifte.⁶⁵
Let not bee knowne the cause wherefore and why,
   hast out of credite thereby our Lawes bee brought:
And sith of custome wee wonted were to lye,
   to tell truthe nowe, at all it profites naught.

But while the rowte of *Sathans* bonde and flocke,
   adreste them selves to gloase and paint this lye:
(*Moegera* comes) and cast her fierye blocke,
   among the heape that all in flames doeth flye.
Then on theyr Captaine, the shorlinges call and knocke,
   but all in vaine, hee coulde not helpe him selfe.
His sinnes had tyed him faster then the rocke,
   hee myght not part out of that woeful delfe.

Then fast upon *Saint Frauncis* gan they crye,
   mee thought as it were a mad Mattins they song:
They were so prickt with paines they had no time to lye,
   the parishe was beguilde, the seconde peale⁶⁶ not rong.
Some song *Sanctamaria Ora pro nobis,*⁶⁷
   with Sensars & Candlestickes they brake cache others face:
The Pope sweare Gods fleshe *Pax vobis,*
   who lost but his labour there was so small grace.

Some cryed on Saint *James,* and some on Saint *John,*
   and some on Saint *Austen,* Saint *Laurence* and *Leo.*
On Saint *Peter* with his Keyes, cryed many a one,
   but among the whole rowte I heard not *Laus deo.*⁶⁸
Suche raye was never hearde, what ever they meant,

---

⁶⁵ Marginal Gloss: The Tree is knowne by his fruite.

⁶⁶ A peal is a summons to church via the use of the bells, usually.

⁶⁷ Holy Mary, pray for us.

⁶⁸ Praise God. Robinson's point in mentioning the Latinate prayers is to highlight that although the rabble in Hell cry out to their Catholic saints in Latin, rather than in the vernacular, they forget to praise God himself.

    the noyse shoke the clowdes that hang in the Skies:
With nailes and teethe, eache others fleshe they rente,
    that *Ecco* reportes the fearefull plaintes and cryes.

But when they see that *Morpheus* kept his place,
    this cursed Captaine fast upon him cryed:
And sayde come *Morpheus* and vewe our woefull case,
    beholde howe I and all my mates bee fried.
No lenger leyn the trueth they might for woe,
    and Maugere[69] of theyr willes *Pluto* them compelde:[70]
Wherfore and why, they urged were to shoe,
    and so at lengthe, these wordes to him hee telde.

I was (quod hee) a Pope and of my name,
    the Sixt I was and *Alexander* hight.
But for to heare my life, no man may bide for shame,
    that hath the dread of God before his sight.
But lende a while thy lystening eares to mee,
    and I shall frieght thy head in bearing of the least:
Sith my rewarde thou doest so perfite see,
    to tell the truth at length I call it best.

In learned Scholes I had beene trayned long,
    and hoyste by fortunes wheele, I was a loftye height:
Yet still my heart in high *Ambition* hong,
    my head for higher state, still practisde sleight.
From highe to harre, I gaped everye howre,
    first calde *Theodore Borgia*[71] of birth and line:

---

[69] Two possible meanings for this word – one meaning, present from the 14th century, is 'and reproach of their wills' but an alternate, more likely use is in the example: 'and a Curse upon II. v. 12 [Fortune] That hath (maugre her spight) thus low me laid in dust their will' as in the sense Spenser uses the term in reference to Fortune (cited in *OED* online, 'maugre').

[70] Marginal Gloss: The Traitour & the theef: both confesse the truth when they see no better.

[71] Marginal Gloss: Theodore Borgia afterwarde made pope and called Alexadre and surnamed the sixth.

A Cardinall I thought not of greatest power,
    yet see my fortune in my later time.

(For as I sayde) from height to harre, yet herte of all,
    I thought to sit, unworthye though I were:
There was so many watching for the balle,
    whose eyes by devillishe arte, I did deceive and bleare.
Many being of mightier birth and blood,
    of greater fame then I by farre awaye,
Woulde have prevented mee with many a snub,
    because I sought the seate, and Papal sea.

And when I sawe I could not reache the marke
    and I wanted power and friendship tooe:
With conjuration I gan to playe my parte,
    and craftlye theyr mindes I altered newe.
Through Nigromncie and Invocation, I
    calde up a Devill with whome I did confarre:
Touching my sute, who aunswered by and by,
    to graunt him his request, hee would exalt mee harre.

Thus being conversaunt with Devilles leng,
    theyr ayde and helpe I craved every daye:
They aunswered mee with speache of pleasaunt tongue,to
doe theyr best they would not sticke nor stayr,
But first I must both covenaunt and vowe,[72]
    in presence of the filthye Prince of darkenesse:
That all his Lawes infernall I shoulde allowe,
    and thereunto addicte my selfe by practise.

Whiche graunted was, and not denyed at all,[73]
    to *Mons Caballus,* a place not distant farre,
In a cleare daye this Prince infernall

---

[72] Marginal Gloss: The promise to the Devill.

[73] Marginal Gloss: Mons Caballus a secrete house to worke knaverye a litle without Rome.

I mette, so close no living body warre,
In a Chambre there, him selfe hee did present
   in Ritche apparell, and Golden rayes to see,
Three crownes upon his head, Orcht with stones Orient:
   lyke statelye robes hath not beene seene with eye.

A seemelye face presenting midle age,
   a stature meete as might bee thought in minde:
His countenaunce shewd, a person verye sage,
   whose wyll to mine, by cruell oathes I joynde.[74]
Thus corporate like Prothonotarie,[75]
   or of the world the greatest Prince of all:
What was it then that I calde unto memorye:
   but it was graunted mee without deniall?

For there hee graunted mee my heartes desire,
   and sayde I should bee Pope the next that was:
When with the Phoenix set my heart on fire,
   suche hast I made to see it brought to passe.
Then with a gladsome heart I wishte to knoe,[76]
   the time of my pontificalitie:
And howe I shoulde in state of conquest goe,
   because I bare a deadlye hate to Italye.

Hee aunswered mee with great disceyte and sayde,[77]
   a leven and eyght I should bee Pope of Rome:
But see at length, howe I was quitie and payde,
   it provde not so when all was sayde and done.

---

[74] Marginal Gloss: Prothonotarie is understande the greatest writer or Clarke in whose likeness the devill shewd himselfe.

[75] Pronotary, *OED* def. 1b: In England: the chief clerk or registrar in the Courts of Chancery, of the Common Pleas, and of the King's or Queen's Bench. Now hist.

[76] Marginal Gloss: Behold the fruites of our holye Father the Pope

[77] Marginal Gloss: The deceytful & doubtful promise made by the deuil to the Cardinall. Robinson is here referring to rumours that Alexander acquired the papacy via simony.

I made accounte to prosper ninetene yeere,[78]
    and glad I was as any man might bee:
I thought to make them stoupe both farre and neere,
    but yet I was deceyvde, the Devill failed mee.

Innocens of that name the tenthe died straight,
    then by the most elections, placed was I:
In the chayre of Pompe, I stretchte my selfe on heyght,
    for Pope I was proclaimed by and by.
Then *Alexander* the sixt I had to name,
    and all for Solemnization of degree:
Thus rechelesse Rome agreed to the same,
    bothe Ritche and Poore, then wishte it so to bee.

Thus was the Myter, with the Triple crowne,
    ouchte rounde about with stones of worthye pryce,
(Set on my headde) in chayre of statelye Rome,
    igraven subtelly by curious crafty vice.
Arayed in robes of glearing beaten Golde,
    with Pearles depotherid here and there in sight:
And at my feete in handes did Cardinals holde,
    a Rose of finest mettall costlye dighte.

I treade on *Tissue,* eache foote I set on grounde,
    above my head was borne a shryne of golde:
Eache knee fell to the earth, to heare my voyce or sounde,
    who went at libertye, that I bad take or holde?
Kinges and Princes, with noble peeres I brought
    in feare and awe so muche, they durst not route,
Them and their countreys I sackt & brought to nought
    to mee and mine that would not bowe and stowpe.

All Italie in my wrathe I rente and shooke,
    all Christian Princes I vexed night and daye:
I banish Kinges, their regall seates I tooke,

---

[78] Marginal Gloss: The devil to the Cardinall.

who durst to mee, so hardye doe or saye.
Honoured like a God I was in every steede.
　　Who spake against my Lawes that scaped death?
All faithfull men with sworde and fire I rid,
　　alleadging that they liv'de out of the Christian faith.

A leven yeeres the Tyrante thus I playde[79]
　　and eyght monethes, then sicke I fell at laste:
I wared feble, my courage quite decayde,
　　I pinde awaye and *Atropos* made haste.
Thus I kept my bedde longe space and time,
　　the cause thereof I gladlye wisht to knoe:
So at the lengthe I calde a man of mine,
　　that of my secreates many times did knoe.

Modena was his name that best I trust,[80]
　　into my Waredroabe, my keyes withall I sent:
There laye a Booke within a Cubbard thrust,
　　of *Nigromancie in Servius* first frequent.
When as my servaunt into my Waredroabe came,
　　(A Pope hee founde) all deckte in Ritche araye:
That seemed as hee thought a very earthly man,
　　Of whome afrayde, my servaunt came his way.

And all a freight to me he tels this tale,
　　which drewe me in a maze and musing minde:
Yet after a while, I calde my man by name,
　　and sent him once againe the booke to finde.
This booke with golde and precious stones was bounde,
　　I never loved Christes Testament halfe so well:
Of Nygromancie there was containde the ground,
　　throughout the earth there was not any such.
But when my man the Wardroabe entered

---

[79] Marginal Gloss: Tyrantes prosper not long.

[80] Marginal Gloss: Popes Munckes Friers &c. in steede of gods word studied Conjuration Nigromacie & other cursed acts.

againe, he founde the Pope jawsting up and downe:
Although he were afrayde, yet manly ventred,
   and fainde himselfe, as though he sought a gowne.
But terriblye this Pope with sparkling looke,
   (sayde to my man) my friende what doest thou here?
Where at hee shranke forgetting of the booke,
   almost hee lost his winde for very dread and feare.

With trembling fleshe anon thus aunswered hee:[81]
   for the Pope I come to fetche a Gowne (hee sayd)
What Pope? (quod vision) you have no Pope but mee,
   and I am hee, that ought to bee obeyde.
With this my man returned backe agayne,
   and what hee sawe revealed in myne eare:
Whiche when I heard did much augment my payne,
   for death at hande, I knew would straight appeare.
Then sicknesse did encrease, eache hower more and more,
   and at the length, time gan to drawe so nye:
One like a messenger rapping at the doore,
   with open mouth awaye dispatche gan crye·
With this the doores abroade gan flye,
   and rushing in hee comes to speake with mee:
First word hee sayde: haste haste dispatche (quod hee)
   the time is come, from death thou canst not flee.

Then objected to his charge full sore,
   the former promise that he made to mee:[82]
Howe I oughte to live eyghte yeere by covenant more:
   And if a leven and eyght observed bee
(Quod hee) agayne my sayinges you have mistaken,
   eleven yeares eyght monethes was all I meant:
My promise to observe I have not yet for saken,
   of eleven yeeres eyght monethes not one doeth want.

---

[81] Marginal Gloss: The aunswere of the messenger to the vision and the answere of the vision againe.

[82] Marginal Gloss: The Pope is deceived by the Devilles craftye promise.

Full glad I woulde have crav'de a lenger time,
    but all was vaine to speake him fayre at all:
With cruell lookes, hee aunswered thou art mine,
    thou shalt with mee, into the lake infernall.
And thus he turnde his backe and went his waye,
    then straight my Corps, did yeld up vitall breath:
My wofull spirite he toke with him that daye,
    where nowe I am tormented with double death.

Loe, what it is to worke by Conjuration,
    or to deale with devils by wicked arte?
Beholde the ende of all abomination,[83]
    am I not well rewarded for my part?
A *Guerdon* meete is Hell, for suche as I,
    that sought so much to sitte in statelye seate:
(Nowe who is Pope) unhappye wretche I trye,
    that am preparde for Sathans hooke a baite.

Loe *Morpheus:* thus I did beginne and ende,[84]
    I lefte my Sonne with all my heapes of treasure:
Through al the world, there was not one his friende,
    poore and ritche still sought his great displeasure.
I lefte his Sister (whome both wee twoo)
    as ofte as pleased us did use and take,[85]
Carnallye eache night and daye wee knewe,
    a common Concubine, I did my Daughter make.

And with these wordes, *Maegaera* commeth flying,
    a thousande newe devised plagues shee bringes:
Take heare (quod shee) your just reward for lying,
    and there withal great flames of fire flynges.
This done, shee then departes a pace,

---

[83] Marginal Gloss: A faire warning for Conjurers & Inchanters &c.

[84] Marginal Gloss: The saying is, a good beginning maks a good ending.

[85] Marginal Gloss: Godlye actes of our holie father the Popes doinges.

to put in use her wanted cancarde nature:
A death it was for to beholde her face,
or else to vewe her vglye monstrous stature.

Where at the rable of all this recheles rancke,
 immediatelye like bedlems sweare and stare·
Into the hollowe hole of gleydes they sancke,
 where furious fiendes, theyr fleshe in peeces tare.
Thus they vanisht, and fled out of our sight,
 with carefull cryes, our ruthful eares they filde:
The pit with clowdes of fearefull irkesome night,
 and dreadful darkenes rounde about was hilde.

Yet many wee behelde, with offeringes and oblations
 that approched nighe, for hast they headlong came:
Frier Rushe bare the Crosse, Clarke of the sessions, [86]
 a member of their Churche, the Popes owne man: [87]
Thousandes came knip knap, pattering on Beades,
 Friars Munkes and Nunnes, came after with hast,
As vowed Pilgrimes, came Wives widowes & Maides,
 of the holye Popes workes the fruites for to tast.

Whome when I sawe, theyr state I did bewaile,
 with teares I steepte a thousand times my face·
Alas, they sought that might not them prevaile,
 the Pope their God, was in a woful case.
Hee broylde in fire, and endlesse woe and paine,
 and all his secte, they tasted of the same:

---

[86] Friar Rush was a legendary figure in German and Scandinavian literature; a devil who disguises himself as a monk to enter people's homes. In 1620 Edward Allde published an anonymous pamphlet called: *The Historie of Frier Rush: hoe he came to a house of Religion to seeke service, and being entertained by the Priors, was first made under Cooke. Being full of pleasant mirth and delight for young people* (1620). Published and Reprinted by Harding and Wright for R. Triphook, 1810. Available on Google Books: http://books.google.co.uk/books?id=-zMJAAAAQAAJ [Date Accessed 20/11/2008].

[87] Marginal Gloss: Frier Rush.

For worldly pleasure, Hell is all theyr gaine,
    Beside on earth an everlasting shame.

Woulde God thought I, in this my drearye dreame,
    my countrey men, were present nowe with me:
To vewe the plagues, where Papistes doe remaine,
    that then they might that filthye fashion flee.
And turne to Christ, which suffered for theyr sake,
    the bloodye butchering Pope for to detest:
In health and wealth theyr prayers for to make,
    to God of might that graunteth our request.

But while that thus, I waylde the want of faith,
    awaye (quod *Morpheus*) Lets packe and get us hence:
Why hearest thou not one gasping for his breathe?
    yea (quod I) but knowe not wel from whence
The wofull noyse doeth come, nor where it is,
    geve mee thy hande (quod hee) and bee not frayd:
It is some Sprite rewarded for his misse,
    Whose carefull cryes, his wicked life bewrayde.

His name his life, his actes that did complaine,
All at fewe wordes heareafter doe remaine.

* * * * *

The Bookes verdicte upon this wicked Pope

O God howe worthy is thy name? Thou art our Lord and King.
As many as confesse the same, to joye thou doest them bring.

And such as doe thy name denye, and rob the of thy glory:
Thou dost confound them by & by, and dashe them out of memory.
All secreates thou dost knowe full wel, no man can hide from thee:
And all that in the earth doeth dwell, or in the heavens bee.

Or in the Seas or stony rockes, from farre thou doest behold
The fowles that scale the skies by flockes, and more then
    can be told.
The infernal lake quakes at thy voice, eache fiend doth
    howle and yel:
And thundreth out an odious noise, when they of the heare
    tell.
O filthie Tiraunt then to thee, (I speake) that tooke in hande
Among us all a God to bee, to rule both Sea and lande.
And heaven where the Lord doeth sit, and Hell where nowe
    thou art:
No doubt thou hadst but litle witte, to playe that theevishe
    part.
It is to Alexander that, with open mouth I crie:
Woe worth the time he spared not, to leade the flocke awrie.
Loe, where he is that rulde the rost, and every kinde of feast:
Whose vaunting tongue would boast, he was a Father blest
As well within the holie throne, as lowe in Stigian Lake:
And that he could both up and downe, bring whome he
    pleasde to take.
Twenty hundreth thousand soules, at Masse he could
    remove:
With sealing of his Bulles and scrowles, or wagging of his
    Glove.
So could he pul them downe from God, when pleased him
    againe:

As thicke as flakie snowe abroade, or mistie dropping Raine.
And thus the wolfe devoured our good, & made us slaves &
    drudges
Sackt our countries, spoylde our bloode, and made us lie
    like snudges.
Kilde our soules and bodies two, deflowred wives and
    maydes:
And kept from us Christs testament new, and gave us bels
    and baides.
Olde rotten rellickes, stockes, and stones, and Ceremonies
    blinde:
With stinking pardons for the nonce, to feede our foolish
    minde.

Thus with his Gods both deafe and dumbe, he tyste us from
  the Lord:
Which sent from heaven Christ his sonne, as scriptures doe
  recorde.
Whose precious bloud hath made us free, from Hell and all
  hir sting
And Hellish Pope from thine and thee, which God his people
  wring.
I yrke to name him any more, and faint within my breast:
Vengance doth upon him rore, the Lorde hath thee detest.
Thy just rewarde among thy mates, with lasting paines is
  quit:
In flashing flames bewayle their states, in dolefull dreade
  they sit.
Yet would they say that with a masse, they could Plegethon
  quenche:
And all the soules that damned were, deliver with a blenche.
And yet themselves lye broyling there, in fire past the
  crownes:
And with their Idoles sweate & sweare, though here they sat
  in throes
Me thinke them fooles that had such skill, in fetching soules
  from hel:
And be compelde against their will, in carefull Cave to dwell.
Sith Italie had cause to joye, at this vile Tyrantes death:
What cause have we to thanke the Lorde, that are restorde
  to fayth:
From bondage now are set at large, and woolves delivered
  fro:
And therefore duetie giveth charge, our thankefull heartes to
  sho.
Lets lift our handes with joyed heart, that living be this time:
That Gods true worde in every part, may florish still and
  shine.
Let Alexander save him selfe, with all his holie skill:

For with his rellickes and such pelfe, [88] he may doe what he will.
No doubt he lyeth there for sport, to passe the time away:
Or else to vewe the greate resort, shat Ladies Psalter saye.
Perhaps that Purgatorie paines, he will to blisse convert:
The sillie soules that there remaines, shall taste no more of smart.
Fie on him fie, and all his mates, the heavens curse him yet:
Of flaming Hell he is the gates, and guide to Stigian pit.
His stincking Masses let him take, and Ceremonies blinde:
Doom Gods a thousand though hee make, according to his minde.
Yet he and they doe perish all, the scripture prooves it plaine:
So doe as many slippe and fall, as to his loare doe leane.
But let us builde upon the rocke, of Christes Gospell pure:
So wee with him amongst his flocke, for ever shall endure.
Where as one God and persons three, be praysed day and night:
And where we shall for ever bee, alwayes within his sight.

---

[88] Stolen goods, spoil (*OED*: Forms: lME-16 pelfe, lME- pelf, 15 pylfe).

The wofull complaint of the monstrous *Emperour Heliogabalus* for spending of his dayes in abhominable whoredome[89]

Syth Morpheus thou art come to take the dewe
    of Plutos kingdome where the wicked guerdon have:
Of all the rest thou ever see or knewe,
    I am the marke to guide the rest from scath·
Loe howe I lye, that earst did florish brave·
    and yet Turinus thinkes he hath much wrong,
I heare him hither, upon the furies rave,
    yet not such cause as I Turinus holde thy tongue

Oh how fickle is the staye of honors hie?
    what doth availe a while to guide the earth?
Th'example plaine appeareth now by me,
    an Emprour once descende of noble birth·
My triple crowne that was abundaunce worth·
    my Scepture sette with Saphirs rich to see:
My sworde that helde in feare such murth
    as never yet was dewde by any eye.

Nor yet the sounde of great renoumed name,
    though all the worlde I helde in feare and awe,
That can excuse the least of blotted blame,
    nor that the Gods at all regarde a strawe.

---

[89] Elyot's *The Image of Governance* provides a detailed discussion of both Turinus and Heliogabalus as examples for King Henry VIII. Elyot claims to be using the *Lives of Alexander Severus* (AD 222-35) and Heliogabalus as his source but Greg Walker shows that it was actually the *Historia Augustae* of Lampridius that he used (pp.240-21). In *The Image of Governance* Heliogabalus's fall is attributed to his favouring of men of low birth (in part) and Elyot expresses particular disdain for the low-born servant Zoticus, and, in Walker's words, 'in associating such low-born counsellors as Zoticus with the tyranny of Heliogabalus [. . .] Elyot was able both to imply his support for the destruction of Cromwell and exorcise some of his own demons with regard to his lack of promotion and favour' (Walker, p.250). After the death of Heliogabalus, Alexander Severus, 'purged his own palace of all the low-born sycophants and hypocrites whom his predecessor had brought' (Elyot) and promised reform and renewal. Heliogabalus was known for his lewd behaviour, disregard for religious practice and promiscuity. He was eventually overthrown and executed by his cousin Alexander Severus and replaced with Vetronius Turinus.

(No *Morpheus* no) who doth offende their lawe·
    although he were ten times as high againe:
Upon the snap they catche him in a flawe,
    their hautie maste flies over borde amaine.

Upon the rocke the shaken Hull is cast,
    that prowdely hoyst hir sayle before on hie·
And so unwares they perish wyth a blast,
    the which before mistrusted not to die.
Then from the stincking gayle the sprite doth flee:
    and as the dunghill secke, hath spent his dayes,
The sillie soule, in bale or blisse shall bee,
    thus vice or vertue hath rewarde alwayes.

Unhappie wretch I was of Rome elect·
    and by consent of all the rulers there,
The noble Senate chose me to protect,
    but when in hande the fearefull sworde I beare,
Not onely Rome, but through the whole Empire,
    I quight forgot my selfe, and place they set me in:
Then did my filthie nature straight appeere,
    the hidden smoke, to flashing flames begin.

For after that I had in hande to rule,
    and that my worde to lose and binde had power,
I brought the Senate to a nother schoole,
    exalting vice much hier then *Pelops* tower.
The Sages grave expulsing every houre,
    new Lordes, new lawes, it did appeare by me:
Thus Rome to ruine I brought from honour,
    from vertue to vice, great shame and infamie.

Thus first of all, when I from *Syria* came,
    to Rome to rule, and royall scepture guide
Heliogabalus:[90] the Romaine bloode may banne,

---

[90] Marginal Gloss: Varius Heliogabalus.

I was a meane to laye their same aside.
Wisdome nor vertue I never might abide,
   In brute and beastlie toyes alwayes I dwelde.
All such as sinne correcte I did deride,
   to filthie living a thousande I compelde.

And thus of Rome that was a mirrour cleare,
   from whome at first all nations knowledge hadde,
Of honour, vertue and prowes the name did beare,
   in myste of filthie slaunder by me was ladde
Whereat the prudent men wept teares full sadde,
   to see the vile abuse that then I set aloft:
Vertuous Virgins then to flie were gladde,
   unravisht fewe scapt, that might be caught.

Insatiable was my swelling luste,
   my pampered fleshe to whoredome was addicte:
I lookte on none but needes consent they must:
   Loe thus (alas) with vice I was afflicte.
I woulde the mortal launce in tender youth had stickte
   my wicked heart that wickednesse desired:
Then should not now no *Plutos* furye prickt
   this soule of mine, that here in flames lyeth fyred.

If Atis chaunce betime I had sustainde,
   then had I squencht the sparke that bred unrest:
My wretched sprite, that nowe in Hell is painde,
   among the Gods in blisse had been possest.
Whom nowe thou seest with torments styll opprest,
   and also scapte on earth, reproche and shame:
Unhappy Rome, then had thou twise been blest,
   that nowe for evermore bewayles the same.

The last *Assirian* King in filthy life,[91]
  I did exceede a thousand kinde of wayes:
All Rome throughout, I ravisht Maide and Wife,
  of Virgins ever, I made them common prayes.
Thus spent I my wicked fleshly dayes,
  I made a *Senate,* of harlottes and bandes:
In open sight I kept no better playes,
  then filthilye to use these common Jades.

Thus houses builded I, for schooles of sin,
  to ayde them with I gave them largely treasure:
The vertuous Matrons, I pluckt them quickly in,
  compelling them unto this filthy pleasure:
(Alas, alas) I past al Godlye measure,
  there was no ho, with mee: who durst denye?
But if they had, I spied such a leasure,
  that from their shoulders, I made their heads to flye.

Into the handes of Bawdes, I did commit,
  the greatest dignitye of the Publike weale:
To common Rybawdes,[92] voyde of grace and witte,
  I gave aucthoritye, aswell to chose as deale,
Who had a sute to mee that did prevaile,
  except in Lechery hee did exceede?
The vertuous sort were ever sure to fayle,
  when as the wicked at every turne did speede.

Luxurious meates and drinckes, I ever sought,
  a thousand wayes I studyed for the same:
Upon the Publike weale the least I thought,
  to labour after lust, that was my game.
If I should publishe halfe by proper name,
  the life of late, I lewdlye led in sinne,

---

[91] Marginal Gloss: Sardanapalus the last Assirian king lived too vile a life to bee rehearsed.

[92] Ribalds, as in *OED* definition 3: A person of abandoned character; a wicked, dissolute, or licentious person. Obs.

The finest head it would both tire and tame,
    therfore to trouble thee, I will not nowe beginne.

What should I speake of noble famous Dukes,[93]
    that from the Senate, by violence I put:
Or of the sage wise Maisters, that with rebukes,
    I cruellye, out of the Senate shut?
I catcht the bitter buske, and lost the pleasaunt Nut,
    twoo Carters I chose to bee my counsell chiefe:
I blindlye drewe to shote at blanked But:
    which was the cause at leangth of all my griefe.

Protogenes the tone of these were calde[94]
    Cordius, thother had by proper name:
These twoo through Rome the common wealth forstald,
    to the losse of my honour, and great increase of shame.
For vice florished, and vertue waxed lame:
    Vitellus[95] in gluttouy, alwayes I did exceede:[96]
Wanton meates for the nonce, then I gan frame,
    to pamper the paunche, when nature list not feede.

What should I tell of the straunge kinde of Fishes,
    so rare uneth no man can knowe them well:
Which at one meale, ten thousand dishes,
    with as many Fowles as doe the Fishe excell,
The like ere nowe, hath any man heard tell?
    an Emperoure to leade (alas) like gluttons life?

---

[93] Marginal Gloss : Yet is nedefull for Princes & noble men to cal sage, wise & learned men to bee of their counsell, & such as bee Gentlemen, well brought up.

[94] Marginal Gloss: Protogenes & Cordius two sleves borne.

[95] Aulus Vitellus (15-69 CE) was Roman emperor in 69 CE and an influentiual leader during the Julio-Claudian dynasty. He is treated with hostility in source materials, possibly unjustly so: 'Hostile sources emphasize Vitellus's gluttony, indolence, and incompetence, though he displayed restraint in dealing with [his enemies]'. *OCD*.

[96] Marginal Gloss: Vitellus at one supper was set ued with 7 thousande fishes, and 5 thousande Fowles.

Yong tender Maides, alwayes I did compell,
 throughout *Italie,* with many a noble wife.

And when I had suffisde by violence,[97]
 my filthye fleshe, yet not contented so:
I ripte theyr wombes in open audience,
 theyr tender bowelles, and secreates for to shoe.
In progresse, when I did delite to goe,
 with mee sixe hundreth Chariots of harlots went:
In steede of Sage, and noble counsels los,
 thus I my time in wickednesse still spent.

And such as chiefe to mee I did appoint,
 and ordaine greatest rule of all to beare:
The sentence of my fame, the villans joynt,
 I innocent, the suters not the neare.
They fed me with follye they whispered in mine eare,
 Zoticus that variette, a slave and dunghill borne:[98]
Whome of nought to noblenes, I did up reare,
 in thende rewarded mee with double scorne.

Hee playde by mee, as *Turinus* did before,
 by noble *Alexander,* who guerdon gave:
(So well) that fame, for evermore,
 soundes up his praise for quiting of that knave.
What should I saye, it is but vaine to rave,
 for in time I had no grace this to prevent:
But hee that will thus much exalt a slave,
 him selfe shalbe the first, that shall repent.

Because this variette, *Zoticus* did excell
 in all wicked vices most abhominable:
I preferde him to the greatest living that fell,
 both Realmes & Kingdoms, with countreys honorable:

---

[97] Marginal Gloss : An abhominable thing and damnable.

[98] Marginal Gloss: : Zoticus

To no man vertuous I seemed conformable,
  but onely to such as abounded in sinne:
To these and such like, I was ever tractable.
  when eache man lost, these knaves did winns.

The Devill so kindled his fire in my breast.
  and fostered in mee such detestable vice:
Because *Alexander* was not slaine, I could not rest.
  that was mine Awntes sonne both learned and wise.
To poyson him I offered, Jewelles of great price,
  because my wickednesse so much hee hated:
One while treason, I conspired with spice,
  in divers drinkes and meates, his death I animated.

But nowe behold the guerdon and rewarde,
  of filthy vile and detestable life:
And howe the Gods theyr servauntes doe regarde,
  defending them from murders bloody knife.
My endeful wel, maye warne both man and wife,
  for *Alexander,* whome I thought to kill:
Hee scapte the snare, when I began to drife,
  the first I was my selfe, that in the same did spyll.

For hee through vertue, wanne the noble heartes,
  of the ancient Senate, and commons of the same:
In whose safegarde, not one from other starles,
  but with consent, togeather joyntly frame.
And thus beganne with mee, that tragicallike game:
  Tyrantes can not raigne, experience long hath taught:
The Gods that suffer long, at length doe blame,
  the wicked imagination, they ever bring to nought.

For by procuring *Alexanders* death.
  I hasted mine owne to my life agreeing:
My wicked servauntes, like Traitours false of faith,
  were thonely conspiratours, and causers of my dying.
They slewe my adherentes, and put mee to flying.
  my familiers a thousand wayes they kilde

Before my face. I standing by and seeing,
   for life durst not speake, but as a coward yeeld.

But how I yeelded, it's shame to make relation,[99]
   I fled into a privie, and there was take,
My mother murdered on the same sorte and fashion,
   Our funeralles togither, amidde that dounge we make.
Loe my rewarde for filthy whoredomes sake.
   The Gods forgot me not, they quitte me home:
They cast me headelong into this fiery lake,
   upon the earth for aye good fame is gone.

(Alas) *Morpheus* yet thou knowst not all,
   I praye thee bide a while and heare the rest,
I am sure as yet, thou never hearde like fall,
   of noble birth, hatcht in so high a nest.
But what prevailes where vice is so possest.
   A while I rulde, and tumbled in my sinne:
I wanted nothing, that mostrous life request,
   of feare I frustrate was, I dred not God a pin.

Therefore mine odious corps throughout the Citie,
   with hookes they drewe, both up and downe the streetes
With ordure fylde, no man of me had pitie,
   haulters of hempe were both our winding sheetes.
Fie on him villaine, they skrickt & cryde like sprites,
   with clapping handes eche one rejoyst to see,
With wordes of great reproche the furies had delites,
   my olde deserved deedes to wreake on mee.

Then to the common Lakes they dregged mee,
   at the filthiest conduict downe they woulde me cast,
But that it was to narrow, at least by fingers three,
   or else I had bene shrinde within that dongue at last.
But then tyed to a mightie mylstone full fast,

---

[99] Marginal Gloss: Semiamira his mother a vicious woman.

into the floode of *Tiber* was I throwne:
Where many a worthy shippe hath past,
    the tumbling streams was made my tumbe and throne.

Loe *Morpheus* loe, thus was I serv'de of such,
    that earst from naught to Princes mates I brought:
Beholde theyr actes, to whome I gave so much,
    above the rest, my misadventures sought:
But alas, the ende of wickednesse is naught,
    the Gods alwayes, take vengeaunce at the length:
I thought I should the fixed starres have raught.
    but yet abated was my hawtye heart and strength.

At the age of one and twentye yeeres I dyed,
    and monstrous *Heliogabalus* they calde my name:
To my reproche, report the same hath cryed,
    who heard therof, that made not sport and game?
And looke who leades my life, shal ever tast the same,
    utter confusion, hasteth for his praye:
Perdurable mischiefe, comes after fast with shame,
    and makes theyr pasporte at the latter daye.

But *Morpheus,* to tell thee all my beastly actes,
    an hundreth Clarkes were not able to pen them:
And againe whosoever should heare of like factes,
    so detestable they are, it would but offend them.
But I praye thee warne thy friendes to amend them,
    my gilte thou hast hard, my paines thou dost see:
To repent betime, I praye God to send them,
    for be sure wicked deedes, are rewarded wickedly.

Bid them flye whoredome, and vile vicious deedes,
    they are sure to loase Gods kingdome for ever:
Honest men doe hate them, as nettles or weedes,
    but shame and ill report leaveth them never.
At length theyr owne Minions doe seeke theyr decaye,
    on whome pursues death, of life the berever:

Which makes an end of beggery, committing Hell the pray,
    if they in wickednesse, unto the ende persever.

And with these wordes this wicked wretche,
    among his tormentes, was toyled so sore,
With a pitifull lookes, his hande forth did stretche,
    as who saye a dewe, I can speake no more.
His mother in a flaming puddle began to roare,
    eche Devill put in use his terrible trade:
With greater spite then accustomed before,
    to terrible to heare the noyse that then they made.

This monstrous Emperour in Hell thus stoode,
    tyed fast by the members on a snakie wheele:
Which ran about as if it were woode,
    Invironde with Bawdes as blacke as the Devyle
Hooked for the nonce with hote glowing steele,
    which Butchered his bowels about his feete:
And for to rewarde his wickednesse weele,
    Th' infernall fire, streight way they beyte.

Whereat anone such smoke there doth arise,
    with leade that boyles, in stormes like raging seas,
And with a twinche, a thousande Dragons flyes,
    ten times as fast as snowe in windie dayes.
Grypes as greedie as Woolves that seeke their prayes,
    and on him gnawe, that myser tyed full fast:
The cruell wheele doth bounce, and never stayes,
    Loe, thus his paines for ever more doth last.

And thus we left this wretch (that dwels in endlesse pain)
A number for to vewe, that crying did complaine.

* * * * *

The Bookes verdicte upon *Heliogabalus*

When filthie lust doth guide, and hath the helme in fist:
Beware the winde and tyde, take heede of had I wist.

A wilfull mate is hee, for to direct the waye:
He doubtes no perill nie, in sayling on the sea.
But hoyse aloft he cries, it blowes a merie blast:
And so at randome flies, while youthfull life will last.
At *Caphars* lampe they runne, with hoysed sayle amaine:
Which seemeth like the Sunne, in sight of feeble braine.
A stale that leades the way, to *Scyllas* sandy cost:
Which drinketh every day, their blood through folly lost.
Charybdis greedie Jawes, lye gaping everie houre:
And whom shee catcheth in hir clawes, shee spares not to devoure.
But loe the prancke of pride, and race that rudenesse runnes:
The ende of wanton workes are spide, se how destruction comes,
Marke rushing youth, how vaine he spendes his retchelesse dayes:
Note well how pleasure breedeth paine, a thowsande kinde of wayes.
If puffing pompe with golde, might ease this Princes paine:
Or force of armed champions bolde, could helpe his griefe againe:
Then all his scrikes and cryes, had quite bene husht and stilde:
So had his eares and eyes, with worldlie workes beene filde.
If I shoulde make rehearse, what his offences were:
Although in prose or verse, it woulde corrupt the eare.
The Gods abhorde his dayes, the worlde doth sounde his shame:
And vengaunce vengaunce manie wayes, agreeth to the same?
What profites now his sporte, wherein he playde the beast,
With all his bawdes resorte, or eke his gluttons feast.
What now availes his crowne, with precious stones beset?
Or and he had as great renowne, as mortall man might get.
Sith mighties know not when, the Goddes will knocke and call,
No more then other poorest men, that simplest be of all,

Therefore looke well about, keepe filthie lust away:
Beware I say the hidden doubt, that lyes in secret sea.
Let vertue guide the helme, and wisdome hoyse the sayle:
So shal you voyde the daungers great, that might your
   voyage quayle.

Young *Tarquine* rewarded for his wickednesse[100]

Awaye with all your playntes and bloobering teares,
Your carefull cryes shut up in silence quite:
For here behoulde such cruelnesse appeers,
Of all the rest but I no wight hath felt the like.
Hell showes hir force on me with double spite,
    No paine to mine, nor none so worthy blame,
    As I deserve, I well confesse the same.

O pryde, pryde, of mischiefe roote and all,
Wo worth the time I thee delighted so:
Thou made me climbe untill I catcht the fall,
Not onely to my shame, but also endlesse wo.
Through pryde, I lost both love, and honor long ago,
    Pryde ruled me so much, no goodnesse I regarded·
    Therefore for wickednesse beholde I am rewarded.

Of noble line and race, descended I,
And a Ruler was, and Ruler mighe have beene,
But yet my heart in wretchednesse did lye:
I fearde not God, nor forst his lawes a pinne,
I ranne my rase alwayes in deadly sinne.
    I cleane forgot my selfe, and eke from whence I came,
    I rather thought my selfe a God then mortall man.

For who, had that, which I did lacke or want,
Of golde or silver or stones of precious price?

---

[100] Tarquin the Proud, or Lucius Tarquinius Superbus (534-510 BCE), was the last of the seven kings of Rome (before the Republic: Romulus, Numa Pompillus, Tullus Hostillus, Ancus Martius, Tarquinius Priscus, Servius Tullius and Tarquinius Superbus). He was reputedly aggressive and tyrannical but according to Polybius he also arranged the first treaty between Carthage and Rome and he completed the temple of Capitoline Jupiter. T. J. Co says that terracottas from the temple at Sant'Omobono (a Church at the bottom of the Capitoline Hill in Rome) show that the later Roman kings modelled themselves on Greek tyrants – which goes some way to proving that his reputation as a tyrant was not entirely fiction: '[his] reputation as a tyrant is not, (or not entirely) a result of secondary elaboration in the annalistic tradition in an artificial attempt to assimilate Rome and Greece' (*OCD*, p. 1475)

For my bodie, costlye apparell was not skant,
Nor nothing else that pryde might well entice,
Thus vertue decayde, but still increased vice.
    To pamper up the paunche, the filthy fleshe fulfill,
    I wholy gave my selfe with earnest heart and will.

Which caused me to acumilate eche houre,
Upon my heade more plagues then can be namde:
The Gods agreed their vengance for to poure
On earth for aye: my name I stainde and shamde,
Thus may you heare how I am justly blamde.
    To my disprayse, and to the prayse of soome,
    That by my losse to honour & great prayse have coome.

Sith *Morpheus* thou art here, and brought thy friend with
    thee
Be witnesse of the woe that *Tarquine* bydeth here:
Sith Poets have pende the wicked life of mee,
Of my rewarde thou mayst reporte well bere.
For the purpose none more meeter then thou here:
    It is no councell that all the worlde doth knoe,
    Nor yet forgot, that was done long agoe.

Fie on rapine, through guilefull treason wrought,
Fie on the swelling flesh that soule and bodie kils:
Fie on filthinesse, whose ende is ever nought,
And fie on folly, that all good maner spils.
Take heede all you that follow fleshly wils.
    Of me prowde *Tarquine* made a mirror clere:
    So may you shunne the paines I suffer here.

Beholde, when I did *Lucrece* finde in bed,
Through harmefull sleight premeditate before,
With naked sworde in hand to hir I sayde:
Consent to me (quoth I) else shalt thou live no more:
Thy tender fleshe this Lance shall carve full sore:
    Then will I slea the worst thy house within,
    Ile make report you were committing sinne.

Which wordes did ravishe so her noble sence and witte,
That tremblingly shee quakes, as doeth the Aspen Leafe:[101]
Feare streight compeld her quakinglye to sit,
Like as shee woulde depart with vitall breath,
The naked Sworde in sight, stil threatning present death,
    Thus I ravisht a Ladye both vertuous and chaste,
    Wherfore I am compelde, (alas) these sorowes to taste.

Whereat eache tongue did talke to my disprayse,
And for the same, I banisht was for ever:
(Sith then) all my posteritie aye evermore decayes.
Loe thus the Gods their vengance doe deliver:
Bewayled be the daye that then I did com thither.
    Among my wicked deedes, this onely was the worst,
    Therefore I was and am for evermore accurst.

I am a sacke of sorrowe in this sincke
And stincking pudole wherein you see me lye:
Whose faultes with mine respondent pende with inke,
Were ever hearde or scande with learned eye?
As vice to my reproache, so vertues Fame doth flye
    Tooth' prayse of *Lucrecia* and example of all such.
    As of hir doe delight, and of me doe reade much.

For when this wilfull act committed was
And I had fed my lust this noble matron on:
Then for to live, nothing she loved lesse,
With wringing handes, Alas she maketh mone,
Come *Atropos* (quoth shee) make hast that I were gone
    And crying still, come *Clotho* come make speede,
    Of *Lucrece* life, untwine the fatall threede.

---

[101] The *OED* quotes from Sir Thomas More, 'If they [women] myghte be suffred to begin ones in the congregacion to fal in disupting those aspen leaves of theirs would never leave waggyng'. In *More Words Ancient and Modern*, Ernest Weekley says, '[i]n the 16th century the female toungue was likened to an aspen-leaf' (Ayer Co Pub: Manchester (NH), 1927, rptn 1971) p.2.

Then pardon craved shee of *Colatine* [102]
And of hir father *Spurius* by and by:
I have made offence, wo woorth the wicked time,
Thus weeping sayde this Lady rufully:
I hearing this from thence departed spedilye.
> And left in wofull plight, this Dame drownd up with teares,
> Whose vertues, in women full rarely now appeares.

But al you Ladies, Wives, and Maides eache one,
Of what degree or yet estate you bee:
No doubte although *Lucrecia* bee gone,[103]
As myrrour maye remaine, this storye when you see.
So may you learne the gifte of chastitye,
> What love you ought your husbandes for to beare,
> In spending of her daies, the profe doeth plaine apeare.

O wretched wight (quod he) howe dare I shewe my face?
The earth doeth threate this wilfull acte of myne:
It is, and wilbe judgde I wanted grace,
Thus losing honour, I steynde my Auncientes line.
At all that beare my name, the people doe repine.
> Yea the very stones that in the streates doe lye,
> Into the Heavens, upon this crime doe crye.

Then wished shee *Ipolas* happye chaunce,
Or *Virgins* ende, or *Didos* long agoe:
(Quod shee) thereof this deede, false Taquine should not vaunce,
That nowe for ever, shame abroade shal bloe
And shall my husband weete him served so?
> That shall hee not, (quod shee) a swoorde shee tooke,
> In blattering blood, the bit all breath forsooke.

---

[102] Marginal Gloss: Colatine was the husband of Lucrece.

[103] Lucretia was raped by Sextus Superbus (son of Tarquinius Superbus) and committed suicide. This led to the Tarquins' banishment by Lucius Junius Brutus, who overthrew Tarquin Superbus and established the Roman Republic (in 509 BCE).

Loe *Morpheus,* alas, nowe have I tolde thee all,
And of my being here, the cause wherefore and whye.
Nowe mayst thou thinke, my grace was very small,
That in my life coulde not for mercye crye.
But wickednesse craves vengeaunce, to the skye.
    And not without a cause the Gods doe punishe hate,
    And so they doe al them that live in whoredome state.

But *Morpheus, Morpheus,* sith thou seest my lot,
A blessed deede it is, the same for to declare:
From Ritche and Poore, I praye the hide it not,
Proclaime howe wicked men rewarded are.
From Pride and whoredome, wishe thy friendes beware·
    The time is short on earth they have to dwell,
    But endles tormentes ever bide in Hell.

If mortall men did knowe, what paine is heare,
Then woulde they lothe the worlde they love so well:
Their pompe, their Pride, and all theyr glittering geare,
To punishe the paunche, some feare would sure compell.
All treason and fleshlye fraude, for to expell.
    All Tyrantes trades no doubte, they would forgoe,
    And if they felt the least of this my woe.

But hee that blinded is, with ease and wealth,
Their ravisht heartes hath dulde their wittes as lead:
Gods feare is gone, and eache man for him selfe,
To purchase pelfe the worldling toyles his head.
The Childe forgettes his Father being dead.
    To taste of death him selfe, no deale mistrust,
    Tyll grizlye ghost do blowe, that needes away he must.

Alas howe vaine is all thing on the earth,
What care to catche, what feare to keepe it still:
What sorrowe it settes, where should bee joye and mirth,
Ingendering hate, there as should bee good will.
Provoking wrath, The verye spirite to spill.

And yet beholde howe everye man doth watche,
And with the trowte the choking hooke doth catche.

And thus farewell nowe gette you hence from mee,
You knowe my minde, deale in it as you will:
My wicked acte, and juste rewarde you see,
And howe my paine increaseth ever still.
Awaye (quod hee) beholde downe yonder hill
   Alecto comes with flaming flashing winges,
   For pride & whoredome, a thousand plagues shee brings.

Then streight departed wee and left him there,
And wandering up and downe, those smokye pittes:
Mee thought a rufull voice, as it a woman were,
Fast bye, declard what plagues shee felt by fittes.
To heare her plaint I almost lost my wittes.
   On whoredome still shee cryed, woe worth that wicked sinne,
   That mortal fleshe so much deliteth in.

But when I calde to minde the leade wherein,
I sawe *Tarquinus* lye, with flames of Brimstone whose:
In middes whereof, hee stoode up to the chinne,
All blubberid with blisters, alas not free one spotte,
And howe with sodden Pitche, his body all was blotte.
   Twoo fiends shot thonderboltes, at him on either side,
   Whereat hee dowkes, his careful face to hide.

Thus in this fornace, amid these boyling heates,
Hee standeth to the Chin, but when hee dowketh soe:
And thus the fezing dartes, ofte in his visage beates,
The feare thereof increaseth double woe.
Thus *Tarquine* was rewarded, and so were thousandes moe.
   That had theyr factes declared to theyr face,
   Which was to late as then, to crye for grace.

The wordes of tormented *Tantalus*, being rewarded for his extortion and couetousnes: Oppressing of the poore people of his Countrey: And for other wicked actes[104]

If any here have cause for to complaine,
What maye I doe that pined am for foode?
I wishe and wante, I crave but all in vaine,
I see the tempting fruite, and so I doe the flood:
Whereof to eate and drinke, I wish none other good,
    If all the world were mine, sharpe hunger gnawes me so,
    To have my belly filde, al this I would forgoe.

No joye nor pleasure, halfe doth glad the heart,
Nor greatest thing that minde hath thought most sweete:
Though all were mine, in every place and parte,
And that eache man were kneeling at my feete,
Like pleasure to this woe, was not compared yet.
    For hunger passeth all, who knewe his part with mee,
    No death so bad, as living thus to bee.

But wickednes want'h not his just reward,[105]
All you that beare rule therefore
Howe you come thereby, it's best you have regard:
And being mighty, how you use the poore.
Your owne infirmityes remember evermore.
    Beware of covetousnes, it's a slye and slieghtye baite[106]
    The father of Hipocrisie, and forger of disceite.

---

[104] Tantalus was the son of Zeus, father of Pelops and Niobe and legendary ruler of Sipylus (a mountain in modern Turkey). Along with Ixion and Sisyphus, Tantalus is one of the archetypal violators of human laws laid down by Zeus. Tantalus was one of the first mortals and so he was allowed to dine with the gods but he stole nectar from the gods to give to his mortal friends and he tried to trick the gods by serving his son Pelops to them at a banquet. His punishment is that he is 'tantalised' with food and drink; it is always in sight but never attainable.

[105] Marginal Gloss: Gregor.

[106] Marginal Gloss: Bernar.

And ambition is a privie poison,
It's also a pestilens, covered closse:
The nourishe of envie, the fountaine of treason,[107]
The mouthe of make bate, to all mens losse,
The blinder of hartes, as the world nowe goes.
    Making of remedies, diseases greate store,[108]
    And of pure salves, many a great sore.

But hee that seekes above the rest to bee,
And gapes to reache the highest starre alofte:[109]
No doubt many times forgetteth equitie,
And also Justice, it plaine appeareth ofte,
Who desireth glorye, that fortune hath not skofte·
    Though lulde a while, within her fichle lappe,
    At length she leaves him cadgde within her cruel trappe.

But al to late alas I doe confesse,
My wicked crimes, wherefore I suffer nowe.
In time and space, I would not finde redresse.
To God nor man, I would not bende nor bowe:
No mans Judgement but mine owne I would allowe.
    Repent that life, I thought I had no neede,
    For as on earth, I thought eache where to speede.

Though for my helpe, confession come to late,[110]
Yet in time, confession is a remedie:
It confoundeth vices, restoreth vertues to eache estate.
Devilles it vanquisheth, in greatest extremitie:
The Gates of Paradise, it openeth most freely.

---

[107] Marginal Gloss: Plutarch.

[108] Marginal Gloss: Hermes.

[109] Marginal Gloss: Tullius [Cicero].

[110] Marginal Gloss: [St] August[ine].

Gods vengeaunce ceasseth, if man confesse betime,[111]
But so to doe, the grace was never mine.

Sith confession is the life of a sinner,[112]
A glorye to good men, and necessary to th' offendour.
Hee that will not confesse, whereof he was beginner,
His grace with mine maye bee called sclender.
But happye is hee that goodes ill gotte doth render
    To them againe, from whence they came at first,
    Bee sure otherwaies they stande to God accurst.

(Alas) how vaine is pleasure, that most so much imbrace?[113]
With what diligence, and expectacion men
Doe seeke this worldly wealth, that bideth but a space?
Sliding stilye hence, no time appointed when,
Wherefore I wishe you all, Gods hasty wrath token:
    Boast not to daye, what thou wilt doe to morrowe,[114]
    Or yet the Sun go down, thy mirth may turne to sorow.

Set little by richesse, and riche shalt thou be,[115]
Set lest by renowme, and fame shall love thee best:
Care not for afflictions, take them quietlie,
Let reason rule thee, so shalt thou be in rest.
He that scapes the wrath of mightie Jove is bles,
    But they that wicked are, no doubt must plagued bee,
    What needeth better proofe, or tryall but by me.[116]

---

[111] Marginal Gloss: [St] Ambrose.

[112] Marginal Gloss: Barnar.

[113] Marginal Gloss: [St] August[ine].

[114] Marginal Gloss: Hierom.

[115] Marginal Gloss: Chrisost.

[116] Marginal Gloss: Seneca.

For judgement without mercie is ever due[117]
To them that be unmercifull to the poore:
But sure mightie men, doe thinke Gods worde not true,
They thinke to line, and dure for evermore,
As I my selfe did, Alas I crye therefore.
  My wicked deedes, my woe doe still increase,
  And puttes me out of doubt, my paines shall never cease.

One day deemeth another from time to time,[118]
Of this, or that, as things doe chaunce to fall:
But the last day giveth judgement, declaring every crime
When eche man is compelde to make accountes for all,
Then sweete worldely welth, doth taste like bitter gall.
  Who hath sustained wrongs, for vengaunce then shall cry.
  Th'oppressors of the poore, shal perish by and by.

And with these wordes, he snatche at the tree,
The fruite whereof, declined to his lippe:
Which on the sodain, from hys mouth gan flee,
And floodes with swelling waves upon his chinne doe hit.
Yet might he not attaine thereof one bit.
  But starving standes, betweene these two for foode:
  Disguisde for want of meate, this careful Caitive stood.

And looking backe by chaunce hee *Morpheus* spyed
(And me) that stoode upon a bancke above:
To whome streight waye hee showted, houlde and cryed,
Come neere good *Morpheus* and see the paines I proove.
And warne all them, to whome thou bearest love,
  My wicked lyfe, that once I ledde to flee:
  Byd them restore the gooddes got wrongfully.

---

[117] Marginal Gloss: Jacobus.

[118] Marginal Gloss: Plinius.

And what's thy name quoth Morpheus woulde I know?
From whence thou came, of whome thou art descended?
And why thou doest endure this cruell woe,
What hast thou done, the Gods be thus offended?
My actes (quoth hee) might well have bene amended.
>But when I was on earth, and had the worlde at will,
>*Lactaneius*,[119]
>I never thought to dye, but to have lived still.

I am the sonne of Jupiter, a God of mightie fame,
And borne of Plote, as witnesse writers olde,
And at my birth had Tantalus to name,
Lorde of many a countrie. I was a Captaine bolde,
But the cause of my plague the Poets have mistolde.
>Yet Morpheus thou shalt here the cause wherfore and why
>The Gods awarde me here to wayle and crye.

Some thinke the Gods tooke vengaunce for my sonne,
Young Pelops, whome when I wanted meate,
And that the Gods unto my house did come,
Because some saye I slewe him for to eate,
The Poets therefore thought that I thys fleeing bayfe,
>Was judged by the Gods always to want & wish:
>(As still I doe) but yet the cause was this:

For in my countrie none but I the cheefe:
Subject unto me they were both far and nie.
Who was so hardie but mauger of his teeth,
I pluckt him on his knees, and if he lookt awry?
But (alas) of wicked counsell each houre may I crye,
>Which put it in my heade, the poore for to subdue
>In Phrigia where I rulde, which now full sore I rue.

---

[119] Lactanius was a fourth century Christian apologist, brought to Nicodemia by the emperor Diocletian. He was later tutor to Constantine I's eldest son Crispus. In the Renaissance he was known as the 'Christian Cicero' because he was considered 'the most classical of all early Christian writers' (*OCD*, p. 811).

What could bee thought, that earthly man might please,
To pompe the paunche, or feede the greedy eye?
(Nothing at all) but by the lande or seas,
With a word of my mouth, I had it by and by.
I thought to mount above the starry skye.
    A woefull chaunce betide, the causers of my smart,
    Which counseld mee to play, the Tyrantes parte.

Alas, alas, what grace had I vile wretche,
To poule, and spoile, my subjectes as I did?[120]
Out of reason, theyr rentes I did both racke and retche:
And another sort from house and grounde I rid:
Compeld them to bandone familye and kinred,
    I banisht whome mee list, eache man was glad to please
    Both mee and mine, that thought to live at ease.

I never had enough, ne could I bee content
To take the world as all my elders did:
I famishte the countrey with fines and double rent.
Esteeming not the mite, that poore men to me offred,
I gapte for gobs of Golde, which greedily I coffred.
    Money was my desire, get it howe I might,
    Of Ritche or Poore, all one, as wel by wrong as right.

But *Morpheus,* nowe to tell the sum and all,[121]
I will not leave the least, for thus it is:
My servauntes through theyr counsell were principall,
That thus I was corrupt, I crye therefore alas,
They fed mee with fables, to bring theyr purpose to passe.
    And in my name the poore they spoyled quite,
    To mee unknowen, when I receiv'de no mite.

Thus many a score, that served mee that time,
That were of base degree, and of the simplest sort:

---

[120] Marginal Gloss: Repentaunce too late.

[121] Marginal Gloss: Wicked counsel.

By title of my name, alofte beganne to clime,
And sought for seates of greater fame and port:
To spoyle my subjectes they thought it but a sport.
    The simplist knave I had, that any office beare,
    Was honored of my Subjectes, as I my selfe it were.

For theyr owne advauntage as it did appeare,
To picke them thankes, within mine eares they whisper,
Keepe down yet dunghil knaves (quoth they) in dread & feare
The Churles bee ritche, let's purge them with a glister:
The poorest widowe, bee sure they never mist her.
    The fatherles, (alas) a begging out they thrust,
    Who payde not al & more, a packing needes they must.

And so my subjectes heartes (alas) I lost,
My honor eke decaide, eache tongue declarde my crime:
Thus I purchaste hate of them that lov'd me most,
And bare the name, for worst of al my line:
Thus were the poore opprest, eache day by mee and mine.
    A thousand hungry soules, within one yeere made I,
    For meate and drinke, the countrey through to crye.

I was corrupt with covetise, I never had enough,
For all my worldly treasure, yet ever was I needye,
As fast as I spoilde, al the countrey through,
Yet with the Cormorant,[122] I gaped alwayes greedye,
Therefore the rewarde of my wickednes came spedye.
    For my extorcion and famishing of the poore,
    Beholde howe I am quitte, with like for evermore.

---

[122] I think he means 'As with the Cormorant' and is referring to the bird: *OED* def. 1: 'large and voracious sea-bird (Phalacrocorax carbo), about 3 feet in length, and of a lustrous black colour, widely diffused over the northern hemisphere and both sides of the Atlantic' and def. 2: 'fig. An insatiably greedy or rapacious person. [. . .] 1531 Thomas Elyot *The Book Named the Governor.* III. xxii, To whiche carmorantes, neither lande, water, ne ayre mought be sufficient'.

Morpheus, move thine acquaintaunce to take good heede
Whome they appoint and put in aucthoritye,
Let them bee sure, they shall aunswere with speede,
For extorting the poore, and other enormitye:
Although they mistrust not, any transformitye.
    But alwayes doe thinke, on the earth for to dwell,
    Unlookte for comes death, and rewardes them ful wel.

Who hated I so ill, as them which lov'de mee best?
Who gained at my handes, but such as taught mee guile?
Those that wishte mee worship, I ever loved least:
My practise was alwaye, my countrey for to spoyle,
By meane whereof I did my name defile,
    And such as would in myne affaires have dyed:
    Moste churlishlye, of thankes I have denyed,

Thus on this worlde, a God I alwayes made,[123]
Wherein I thought to dwell for evermore:
At my pleasure and will, the Countrey did invade:
Passing not a pinne for the curses of the poore.
If hee filde not my bagges, I thrust him out of doore,
    As for mercye, at my hande, it booted not to crave,
    They did but sturre my choler, more cruelly to rave.

I lov'de *Vaineglory* most, hee was my counsel chiefe,[124]
And *Private Gaine* of whome I spake before,
And other such, as teare my subjectes with theyr teeth,
As a Dogge a bone, they usde my people poore,
Of *Telales* and *Pickthanks*, I alwayes had great store,
    Whose whispering tales, were Gospels in mine head,
    And thus in steede of trueth, with falsehood was I fed.

My shoulders laden were, with worldly muck,
And yet mine eyes desired what I see:

---

[123] Marginal Gloss: Too many of this condicion at these daies.

[124] Marignal Gloss: There wantes no pickthanks.

Though all the world were layde upon a rocke
It never might have satisfied myne eye,
If more then inough, had halfe contented mee,
   I might have liv'de, in honour al my dayes,
   And of the poore have wonne immortal praise.

But fye of worldly mucke, fie on it twenty times,[125]
To mutuall envie, most men it doeth provoke
And vaineglorye, doeth teache a thousand careful crimes,
In every mischiefe, these twee, doe ever strike a stroke,
A deceytfull sweetenesse, That bindes to Sathans yoke[126]
   An unfruiteful labour, a continuall dread and feare,
   A daungerous advauncement, The aucthor of dispaire.

Vaineglory alwayes, without repentaunce endeth.
Whose beginning without providence is:
Provokes the Gods to wrath, the people it offendeth.
Who gloreth in this globe, that thinkes hee doeth amisse?[127]
Hee gapeth like a glutton, for glorye to bee his,
   Whose eyes bee fixte into the Skies on hye,
   And wisheth winges above the Sunne to flee.

What greater follic can bee then to covet Ritches,[128]
It tormentes the minde, and breakes the quiete sleepes,
It vexeth the heart, and myrth away it twitchis.
Many miserable thoughtes, in the conscience it keepes,
It shakes up the stomacke, making sowers of sweetes,
   It shorteneth the life, as the Philosopher sayeth,
   It makes Children, & kinsfolke, wishers of your death.

---

[125] Maringal Gloss: Paulus.

[126] Marignal Gloss: [St] Augustine.

[127] Marginal Gloss: Such there are.

[128] Marginal Gloss: Diogenes.

It keepeth from doing Godlye charitable deedes;[129]
It causeth the partye not cherishe him selfe,
Being never friendly to any man that needes,
Dispatching eache man of theyr perfite health,
Loe, these bee the fruites of this vile worldly pelfe,
    Which causeth man, to live a misers life,
    Whose ende is destruction, to man, mayde, and wife.

And with these wordes, the woefull sillye wretche
His Jawes ope caste, that boilde and burnde with heate:
And withered starven armes, with violence doe stretche,
    eate,
In hope to catche the slieghty tempting bayte,
Which hanges on flattering bowes, that flatters him to
    And to his mozid mouth declines yet barked is ful drye,
    When the hungry soule, would eate, away yet [the] fruite
    doth flye.

And flood on every side, swels up with boyling waves,
Wherein hee standes an inche above the Chinne:
Whose cruell thyrst to drynke, no litle craves,
But when to taste, poore soule hee doth beginne,
It blencheth out of sight, as it had never beene.
    Then touched fruite, doeth beate him on the teethe,
    Appointed by the Gods, to worke him double griefe,

With face deformde, al quaking standeth hee,
Ten times worse then death, the Caitife[130] lookes:
Nought els uppon his legges, but skinne and bones to see,
Eache finger of his hande, as bare as angling hookes,
His bellye as thinne, as out of season flowkes.
    Muche like a shadowe of the Moone hee standes,
    With rewfull cheare, doth wring his careful handes.

---

[129] Marginal Gloss: Horace.

[130] Prisoner.

And after a while, amid his tormentes greate,
(Quoth hee) Oh *Marcus Curius,* blessed bee thy dayes.[131]
Thou wast indifferent, thou dealt not with disceate·
Thou wanst thy subjects harts, & wanst immortal praise:
Thou wast a loving Capitaine, to men at al assaies.
    For to thy people thou wast a Parent deare,
    As by thy noble actes, among them did appeare.

Thou didst devide the soyle, by just and equall line,
And to eache man, thou fortye acres gave:
Which ground before alotted was for thine.
Yet like, for like, with least thou would but have,
The faithful heartes of men, was al that thou didst crave.
    Therefore thy just rewarde, is with the Gods on hye,
    And through the earth, thy same, abroade doth flye.

And wride his head, and *Morpheus* straight behelde,
Thou knowest my name (quoth he) I pray yet get the hence
To leave my talke, by thyrst I am compelde:
The hungry worme, doth also worke mee vengeance.
Sith of my deedes thou hast true intelligence,
    Declare it to thy frindes, how ever they regard it,
    How I for my wickednesse of *Pluto* am rewarded.

That will I doe (quoth he) the best I may or can,
To all the worlde divolgat shall it be,
My voyce shall thunder it out unto eche man,
The rewarde of wickednesse that now I see:
Doe so (quod *Tantalus*) and there with all doth hee
    Betwixt the fruite and guylefull fountaines vaine,
    Watching wisheth foode to ease his hungry paine.

And thus we both departe, and went our way,
This dreirye doubtfull Myser, left we there,

---

[131] Marginal Gloss: Marcus Curius.

Whose thirste increaseth griefe, to see the pray
That heart woulde have, in sight doth aye appeere.
Streight came *Alecto,* And shee began to sweare:
   (quoth shee) thou oppressor, thy hunger still increase,
   To rewarde thy wickednesse, hope not to have release·

No sooner from the valley were we gone,
But in our eares we hearde a carefull crye,
Which sayde (alas) in *Plutos* kingdome none
Sustaineth halfe the plagues that I doe taste and trye,
Fie one worldely workes, fye upon them fye.
   (Quoth *Morpheus*) to me, make haste, we will go see,
   Who it is that plaines and mones so grievouslye.

* * * * *

The Bookes verdicte upon *Tantalus*

The monstrous Camel, that stamping beast, & cake the
   sluggish Asse
And Bayarde bolde, I may compare to many men alas·
Which with the Camell beares awaye, the massie packe of
   pelfe,
Yet twise as slowe as sluggish Asse, but onely for themselfe.
The lothsome loade of wished wealth, the harts hath so
   bewitcht:
That Justice, friendship, pitie, and love, away is from them
   twitcht.
With brags they bouldly leape & plunge, nothing they do
   mistrust:

As *Baiard* doeth,[132] till at the length, to yeld to harme they
   must.

---

[132] Bayard/ Baiardo, from Ludovico Ariosto's *Orlando Furioso*; Rinaldo gives Ariosto a horse called Bairdo and Chaucer uses this as a common name for a horse; e.g. *Troilus and Cresyde* I. 218 'As proud Bayard gynnyth for to skippe Out of the wey'. The *OED* also cites a reference from Thomas More for 'Bayard': def. 2:c. 'Alluded to in many phrases and proverbial sayings, the origin of which was in later times forgotten, and

These Beastes mee thinke doe wel present, the qualities of such,
That with the *Camel,* drug and drawe, of worldlye wealth so much.
As *Tantalus* the *Phrigion* did, the *Camels* part that plaide.
Whose mind from *Midas* muck, in time, no counsel could have staid.
His Beastly heart beare that away, that body nor bones could doe:
As some such *Camels* at these daies, are lately start up newe.
Within the circuite of our soile, which members beare of men,
Whose customes in their countrey is, to beastly now and then.
For oft their greedy paunche devoures, their neighbors house & ground,
Yea Pastures, Parks, whole fields, & Tounes, & al that may be found.
Which passeth beast, or beastly bones, of worldlinges for to beare:
Although their hearts do crave as much, as both they see and heare.
They hoke and holde, with tothe and naile, by slight of wily braine,
That which we see, each time and tide, doth waste like snow in raine.
Goodes are ill gotte, which causeth losse, of endlesse joy and blisse,
To purchase paines, where lasting griefe, and tormente ever is.
Marke this wel you mighties whome, the Lord appointes to rule,

---

'Bayard' as the type of blindness or blind recklessness – as when Thomas More writes: in 1532 *Confut. Tindale Wks.* 500/1 Bee bolde vpon it lyke blynde bayarde'.

Lende not your eares in any wise, to Peter Pickthankes
 schole.
His flattering fetche doth robbe you al, of famous honour
 due,
Whose painting pensels evermore, reprocheful colours hewe.
And causeth curses of the poore, whose plaints the Lord
 doeth heare,
Redressing streight their care & grief, throughout the earth
 echewhere
That *Camell* then more covetous, what *Asse* more dull of
 witte,
What boulder *Bayara* can be found, to keepe the lothsome
 pitte,
There are these muckserapers at these daies, that swalow
 up the poore,
Which have to much, yet not content, but proule for more &
 more?
Whose gluttons eies are never filde, till gaping chappes bee
 full
Of suddie soile, and slimie slitche, where at this while you
 pull:
And then your woeful soules bewaile, the daies your
 carkasse spende,·
In wickednes, and never could finde any time to mende.
But wordes are wind, what will you more? No vertue is
 regarded:
Be as be maie, the daie will come, your workes will bee
 rewarded.

The rewarde of an Ambicious and vaine glorious counseller, called *Vetronius Turinus*: For his wicked life among them that hee might overcome, and for his Pride: whose wordes folow in the middes of his tormentes[133]

Peace Tantalus hold still thy plainting chaps.[134]
Bewaile no more thy state, thy lot is light enough,
And if thou knewe of my mischaunsed haps,
And how I am torment, within this stinking clough.
    Contented would thou be, where now thou art not so,
    And if thou felte but least of this my endles woe.

Fye of the face of fortunes smiling lookes,
Whose slye deceyte is sugred baytes to cast:
The foolishe sorte to catche upon hir hookes,
That erste from smiling mouth, the *Judas* kisse had taste.
    And suche as shee hath set the hext of all,
    Shee most delites to give the greatest fall.

Who sittes so sure as in the simple seate?
Who is so Ritche, as hee that reason doth content?
Who scapes the hooke, that leapes at every baite?
Who meddles much at last that is not shent?
    Or yet who deales with craft that is not spide?

---

[133] Robinson's source for this material probably comes from Sir Thomas Elyot's *The Image of Governance*, which begins by telling the reader the didactic value of examples of past offences and punishments for the present. He begins with the example of Alexander Severus (who appears frequently in Robinson's poem), under whom Turinus was employed. Showing how Elyot uses images of bad governance to make an ironic comment on Henry VIII's 'slide into tyranny' Greg Walker summarises Elyot's discussion of Turinus: 'There was in Alexander's service, [. . .] an ambitious and vainglorious counsellor", whose corrupt practices the Emperor eventually discovered and punished condignly. Indeed it is his punishment that is the point of the story, for as the text goes on to explain, this counsellor, one Vetronius Turinus, was subjected to a torment that might initially strike readers as "over vehement and grievous" but it would prove upon fuller explanation that the Emperor's said rigour in judgment was necessarily used' (Walker, p. 250; see pp. 247-256 for Walker's discussion of Elyot's use of Turinus's example). Details of Zoticus (who at various points in Robinson's poem and features as a main participant in the fall of Heliogabalus) are also important to Elyot's lesson.

[134] 'plainting chaps', praying lips.

Who hath not al mens wrath, that evermore hath lide?
The sure pathe I never founde as yet,
Which was to set all worldly thinges at nought.
With *Phaeton,*[135] I thought above the starres to sit,
On worldly wealth was evermore my thought.[136]
    But custome teacheth al thinges shal litle bee,
    That to the show semes greate, too worldly eye.

Who dwelles in Princes favours that knowes him selfe,
Or at the least for gettes not what he was?
Who lookes not hye, that catcheth worldly wealth,
Which slippes away as dewe upon the grasse.[137]
    Fye, on it fye, it leades to endles fire,
    And meare destruction bringes, on them that it desire.

But in valleys lowe, the quietst dwelling is,
On loftye mountaines, the storming blast doth blowe:
The mounting *Phenix,* shall witnesse bee of this,[138]
Who doth full well, the heartes of climbers showe.
    Whose ende with her, doth meare destruction call,
    Which doth from loftye skyes, belowe to ashes fal.

Who with *Icarus*[139] seemes to flye a lofte,
Or with the *Pine,* his fellowes overgrowes,
That many times, with fortune is not skofte,
And with the *Pine,* be rente and spoilde of bowes?
    Who standeth in conceyte, with folishe fonde *Nessus,*
    That in the ende of his misfortune misses?

---

[135] Son of Helois (the Sun-God) and Clymene. He asked to drive the sun-chariot for a day and Zeus had to kill him with a thunderbolt because he was in danger of setting the earth ablaze.

[136] Marginal Gloss: Isiodorus.

[137] Marginal Gloss: Hermes.

[138] Marginal Gloss: Phoenix.

[139] Icarus, son of Daedalus. When Minos imprisoned Daedalus he made his escape via the waxen wings. Icarus flew too close to the sun, melted his wings and was killed. Deadalus made is safely to Sicily. *OCD.*

But what availde the Bookes that I have read?
The wicked ende of none, might cause mee to amende:
I sawe long syth, howe every Tyrant spead,
By worthy writers, wose actes had Clerkly pende.
    And theyr succes, that in such vice abounded,
    Howe short they rainde, and were by God confounded.

But let me bee, for so I maye no doubte,
Full well be made a mirrour to each one:
That be in Princes favour, & make them selves so stout,
(As I) unhappy wretch, have beene not long a gone.
    I had so deepe a witte to purchase worldly wealth,
    In vertue a very foole, and cleane deceivde my selfe.

And with these wordes his paines so much encreaste,
That worse then mad, a thousand times he flinges:
Then to the brinke of loathsome lake hee preste,
And cryed, behold, what wicked doinges bringes.
    Drawe neare good *Morpheus,* harken what I saye,
    And to thy friendes report another daye.

I was (quoth hee) advaunste to such degree,
And in the favour stoode, of *Alexanders* grace:
So much at last, that in all causes hee
Looke mine advise, in thinges that doubtful was.
    My counsell lead him, ever as my list,
    Who had a sute, I not his friende, his purpose mist.

All men gave place, when I in counsell close,
Unto this noble Emperoure, both night and day:
My fame eache howre, encreased styl and rose,
I saved whome my list, agayne I put awaye
    (Whome pleased mee) and ruled mee at will,
    I made both good, and bad, full glad to please mee still.

THE REWARDE OF WICKEDNESSE

Vetronius Turinus, is my proper name,[140]
Chiefe counseller, this famous Emprour too:
Which bleard my inward eyes in tasting of the same,
I could not know my selfe, as I was wont to doe.
    Such incomparable sweetnesse, is found in Princes favor,
    Whom Fortune calles so high, forgets their owne behaviour.

Such hap a while exceedeth *Loios* taste,
Whose sinatch some lickoras lips, the most doe wishe:
Yet whosoever to gape, therefore doth haste
Sal trye in th' ende, *Serdonia,* plaine it is.
    For sweetest meates, soure sauce they saye is best,
    This is, and evermore, was used at eache feast.

Thus I elect, and chosen chiefe of all,
In secreate familiaritie, with this noble man:
I was so pufte with pride, I did mistrust no fall,
Thus eache mans heart, through dread and feare I wan.
    A while I plaide the Beare, I nipt both yong and olde,
    I kept them so in awe, to barke none durst bee bolde.

Thus every man of mee did stand in feare,
Eache one with bending knees, to me did bowe:
They honoured mee, as I the Emproure were,
I gaped for such glory, as was not meete nor dew.
    Thus like a chowgh, depaint in peacoks tayles,
    Amid the gulfe of *Scylla,* I hoyst my rotten sayles.

And at the length this one thing blinded me,
When every man my lawfull favour sought,
Then I began to looke both stowte and hie,
I spake them fayre, when inwarde ill I thought.
    Great bribes I did receyve, and made all men beleeve,
    That whome my list, I coulde both gladde and grieve.

---

[140] Marginal Gloss: Vetronius Turinus.

Thus ritche I made my selfe, and most men poore,
That to this noble Emproure any sute procurde:
And those of whome the Emproure made a store,
Such meanes I wrought, that long he not indurde.
    And yet a greater sleyght then this I used long,
    I dayly sought to wrest all men with wrong.

Faire wordes I fedde them with, and nothing elles,
On eyther part their money I receyved,
I eate their kirnels, and fed them with the sHelles.
Who trusted me that scaped undeceyved?
    I playde the Mariner, that looketh backe and rowes,
    And yet with floode, his boate contrarie flowes.

For where these suters did awayte to knowe,
By me this noble Emperour his pleasure,
Then would I nodde my head, and frindely countenaunce showe.
(As who shoulde saye) abyde a nother leysure.
    Thus of the Emprours grave determination,
    I made a trade as twere an occupation.

Till at the length, all men with murmuration,
Perceyving that I fabled with them so,
With open Jawes, made open exclamation,
And earnest lookes cast on me too and fro,
    Whereat report, a Poste did sende for Fame,
    Which causd hir crooked Trumpets sound abrode the same.

Thus to this noble Princes eares at length it came,
And publisht all abroade, it was on every side.
And of the same accusde of every man,
That rounde about me stoode, and to the Emprour cryde:
    O famous noble prince, incline thine eares to heare.
    Turinus wickednesse, to thee shall now appeare.

Then all my former lyfe disclosed was,
And proovde by credible persons before my face:
When the Emperour understoode both more and les,
He judgde me to be led into the market place.
    Where straungers were of countries far and nye,
    Which grievde me worse, then twentie times to die.

In the market place, sometime where I with pryde,
More like a Prince then otherwise had walkd the stones
There to a stake, my limbes full fast they tyde,
With cruell engins invented for the nonce,
    Where young and olde, stoode rounde about to see,
    The fall of him, which earst did looke full hie.

Then hidden malice did shewe his furious face,
Whose tongues before as sweete as suger seemde:
(And crying sayde) thou Tyraunt voyde of grace,
The proofe is plaine, it was not as thou weende,
    Thou thought thou had our harts, because we capt and kneelde,
    Which inwardely with spitefull hate we steelde.

Then curses blacke into the skies they sende,[141]
To all the Gods where mightie Jove doth sitte,
That after all this shame, I might be torne and rent,
Within the puddle of *Plutos* stincking pitte.
    And there withall, their handes a pace they clappe,
    Greene stickes and stubble, about the stake they wrap,

And fire thereto, on every side they set,
Whose powdering smoke, mountes up the loftie skies,
The flashing flame eche man was prone to let,
To th'ende thereby my doubled paine might rise,
    Thus lingered life, with tormentes worse then death,
    By meanes of smoke compelde to yelde my breath.

---

[141] Marginal Gloss: His execution maketh people glad.

Whereat with gladsome heartes rejoyced many a one,
Tooth' great reproche of all my bloode and line,
With hast a Bedle Th' emperour calde on,
And straightly chargde, about the stake that time,
    To sounde these wordes in th'eares of young and olde,
    With fumes lo here he dieth, that fumes hath ever solde.

Thus confusion my guerdon quitte ful well,
And payde my hyre which I deserved best,
The Gods also condemnde me into Hell,
Among the wicked sorte with whome I am possest,
    Of irkesome Stigion whereas *Phlegethons* flames,
    The pompe of cruell Tyrauntes ever dayly tames.

Loe this the lotte of wicked life in th'ende,
Looke to your states you that Counsellors bee,
You that perswade the nobles to offende,
Leave of betime for my rewarde you see,
    Bee sure whosoever in wickednesse proceedes,
    In thende the Gods doe recompence their deedes.

How sayst thou *Morpheus* hast thou hearde the like?
Whome hast thou knowne to have a fall like mine?
Coulde *Fortune* worke to me a greater spite,
Then first to whirle me up, then cast me downe in fine,
    When least of all hir wrath I did mistrust?
    From hext of *Pelops* turret, no helpe but downe I must.

Thus through the coste I got eche poore mans curse,
With shamefull death, and Hell at latter daye:
A deere bought treasure, thus to fill my purse,
To lose the joyes among the Goddes for aye.
    These words no sooner sayd, so much increast his pains
    His tongue with ruful voyce his perfit talke constrains.

This sincke of sorrow wherein he standes and cryes,
With pitche and Brimstone boyles up like a floode,

Where serpents with their triple heads still yelling flyes,
Whose crooked clawes are bathed in his bloode.
   From out whose mouthes such foming flames arise,
   Which lighteth in his face, or spowteth in his eyes.

Eche finger of his hande was turnde to ougly snakes,[142]
His teeth were chaungde to wormes *Cerestres* like:
His legges all serpentes, that dayly vengaunce takes,
Upon eche other, that venomly gan smite.
   His toes upon his feets, were filthie Todes to see,
   That swelde with poyson as bigge as they might bee,

His heart the Captaine of his sleyghtie tongue,
Transformd in likenesse of a Hedgehogge kinde:
Before whose greedie mouth such riped fruite was hong,
As monstrous beast in hearte did wishe to finde.
   Which when he toucht, they turnde to Scorpions all,
   Perforce his lippes from gaping chappes lets fall.

His guilefull tongue was turnde to Crocadyle,
Amidde whose sleightie heade brast out consuming coles,
From out whose eyes fell droppes like gaddes of steele,
Wherewith sometime he trapt poore sillie soules.
   And molten golde into his mouth was pourde,
   Whose gasping gummes most greedely devourde.

And yet a greater griefe then this hadde hee,
A plagie paine above the rest no doubt:
An horrible feend, none such in Hell to see,
Before him standes, whose voyce doth roare and shoute,
   What joyes among the Gods they lose that wicked are,
   This ougly Geylor to him streight did declare.[143]

---

[142] Marginal Gloss: A man deformed.

[143] Marginal Gloss: The scripture alleaged then. Psal. 84. Psal. 24. Psal. 3.

And with the Psalmes began this cruell Clarke,
To taunte the torment wretche with griefe to heare,
Saying *Turinus* incline thine eare and harke:
I am thy Curate, thou art my Parishner.
    Give eare (quoth hee) and marke my sayinges well,
    Else shal these hookes, with care thy corps compel.

And then these places of scripture straight hee reades,
And shakes his Snakie head, with grinning teeth:[144]
And scoffes him still, with all his olde done deedes,
That then to heare, no litle was his greefe.
    And then this frouning Curate, braggingly gan hoast,
    And tels the wretch, what endles joyes hee lost.

Thou hast lost (quoth hee) myrth out of measure,
'All libertye, all Light, all rejoysing and health:[145]
All wealth, all joye, and glorious pleasure,
All honour, all power, al long of thy selfe.
    With solace, and love, unitie, concorde, and peace,
    Wisedom, vertuous melodye, and felicities increase.

'Meekenes, and beatitude, from the is fled and gone,
And that in most glorious heavenly Citye:
Hope for no redresse, be sure heare is none,
But ever more, unspeakeable miserye.
    This Den (quoth hee), is still the place of paines,
    For thee and such, of whom the poore complaines.

'Nowe hast thou lost the company of Archangels,
With Th' apostles, Patriarkes, and Cherubins: , Powers,
Thrones, Dominione, and Aungels,
Confessors, Virgins, Martyrs, with blessed Zeraphins.

---

[144] Marginal Gloss: Roma 8. Apoca. 22. Math 24. 1. Thes. 4. Math 25. Apoca. 7. Apoca. 4. Apoca. 21.

[145] Marginal Gloss: Esay. 43. Esay. 1. Esay. 5. Math. 11. John. 3. John. 5. Luke. 5.

Where righteous sprites, cease not, but always sing.
Holy, Holy, Holy, God of earth, and heaven King'.

And with these words, with hast hee shut the booke,
To some place else hee ranne to execute his spite:
Whereat *Turine* cast up a woeful looke.
(Quoth hee) good *Morpheus* take foorth thy pen and write,
   (Alas) regester up my rewfull wicked ende.
   It may prevent much harme, & if the same were pende.

But *Morpheus* casting downe his heade for woe,
Uneth one worde, coulde well pronounce almost,
But sayd, come *Robinson,* I praye thee let us goe,
My heart doth warche to see this grislye ghost.
   And then he wisht that all offenders see,
   How *Pluto* doth rewarde all them that wicked bee.

And thus we left *Turinus* in his paines,
Whose wante of grace, we both lamented much:
And there in Jayle he shakes his lincked chaines,
Whose bandes to breake, no mortall handes may tuch.
   His endlesse paines it bootes not to be wayle.
   No sacrifice to Jove, can ought at all prevayle.

* * * * *

The Bookes verdicte upon *Turinus*

Loe thus to see him pulde, with raging hagges of Hell,
That whilom thousandes ruide, esteemd with Princes well.
I mervell in my minde, such men should plagued bee,
Whome Fortune hath assinde, unto such dignitie.
But now I doe perceyve, none such the Gods will spare:
That poore men doe bereave, of money goodes or ware.
Or whome by counsell seemes, to blinde their Noble eyes:
Whose judgements best esteemes, and quites with double
   fees.
Or such as sentence sel, by slye and cloked craft:
And harmelesse soules compel, a fruitelesse tree to grafte.

On these the Gods doe poure, their wrath by whole consent:
And alter in an houre, the wickeds yll intent.
Regarding not at all, their statelie hie degree:
But shortlye give the fall to such as climbe to hie.
Turinus now hath lost his prince that lov'de him best:
And such as hate him most, joyde thus to see him drest.
What profittes blubbred teares? The Gods have judged thee:
How long or fewe yeres, (they know) so doe not wee.
To leave thee in thy paines, of very force I must:
No hope but this remaines, a warning fayre I trust.

The two *Judges* for slaundering of *Susanna*: and bearing false witnesse against hir, be rewarded for the same most terribly[146]

Fyrst to this place when happed us to hytte,
A roome we founde where best we myght beholde
Of every side that stinking Stygion pitte,
That all the rest excelde a thousande folde,
Stuft full to'th top it was of young and olde,
    (But as I sayde before) a couple there we see,
    Whose tongues behind were halde with hookes full hie.

Before their faces with trumpet hoarse and dimme,
To powting mouth a monster fell doth set,
Whose voyce increaseth care that be the hearing in,
With foming jawe, his teeth beginnes to whet.
His gloring eyes with sparkes of fire fret,
    He casteth under clowdes, and stints his trumpet streite,
    And with a ratling speech declares these words on heite.

(Quoth he) sith slaunder is committed to my charge,
And that it pleaseth Pluto my service to accept,
Within this pitte mine office wide and large,
His lawes and statutes streight shall be full truely kept.
And there withall aloft anon he lept,

---

[146] The story of the two judges of Susanna can be found in chapter thirteen of the Book of Daniel. This chapter was excluded from Protestant bibles and included in the *Apocrypha*. John Day and William Ceres printed Richard Taverner's edition of the *Apocrypha* in 1549 (STC 2087.5) revised by Edmund Becke, and later published again by John Day in his folio Bible of 1551 (STC 2088). Robert Greene's *A Mirror of Modesty* (1584) claims that he was asked to detail the story of Susanna, 'more largely than it is written in the Apocrypha' (Letter to the Reader). He included details of her life and tragedy in his *Mirror* and dedicated his text to Lady Margaret, Countess of Derby. Greene's text was printed by the printer Robert Ward, who printed Robinson's *A Golden Mirrour* posthumously in 1589 (STC 21121.5).

From the gibbet cuts their tongues wherby they hange,
And like a madde man in a rage into a furnasse flange.

Where molten brasse doth boyle as redde as gleedes,
I blende with sulfer, pitche and stincking tarre,
And scaldes the scoffered tongues that wounded bleedes.
Whose fyring streame may well be spied a farre,
From bottome low which mounth from height to harre.
    And dims the christall skies, & beames of glering light,
    But that we stoode so nie else had we lost the sight.

Tartarus hath this pitte to proper name,
Which is in Hell[147] most yrksome place indeede,
And is appoynted wicked tongues to tame,
That doe delight in sclaunders to proceede,
Who brueth bate that well doth after speede?
    Who staines the vertuous man by false surmised way
    That in the ende least pennie doth not paye?

For mightie Jove that doth in heavens sitte,
To forge commaundes Vulcanus fast to hye,
Newe thundring boltes to make for every pitte,
Whereas these slaundrous wretched verlottes lie.
Who many thousands wrought, and downe sende by & by,
    Which boltes the cruell Jaylor in sturdy Bow doth set,
    And cruelly flinges, with heades full sharpe iwhet.

Into the mouth and through the tongues they flie,
Of eyther of these lyther slaunderous mates:
Where as consuming coales as red as serpents eye,
Doe ever lodge as porters of the gates,
Two serpentes ever sate upon their pelled pates.
    And ever through the skull they pell the braine,
    Yet alwayes as it wasted it still increast againe.

---

[147] Marginal Gloss: Tartarus.

In shooting thunderboltes and arrowes as I saide,
At these false accusers, and breeders of unrest,
That ougly Geylor chaunst holde up his heade,
And *Morpheus* spide, whome then he did request,
To come and see how lyers there were drest.
   For this the place (quod hee) that slaunder doth reward,
   Though many thousandes not the same regard.

And then with filthy forke their jawes abroade he set,
Within whose mouthes were broodes of scorpions hatcht,
Whose hunger not slackt but they might alwayes get
Some part of wicked lime, thus at his tongue they snatch:
And yet it doth encrease, their greedie guttes to hatche.
   Yet they bee never filde, nor hee consumde no deale,
   Loe, thus they taste of woe, that sclanderous lyes do tel.

I saye come neare, this Jayler sayd againe,
And what thou seest among thy friendes report:
Though sclaunder bee torment with double paine,
Yet every daye thou seest I have resorte:
No doubte I trowe, they thinke it but a sporte.
   For els theyr tongues from lyes they would applie,
   To mightie *Joue* they ought for mercye crye.

For if they doe not mende in haste, bee sure
I will mine office yeeld (quoth hee) no double:
Elles a larger dominion, I meane for to procure,
For this is full you see, already round about:
And now such sclanderers come, that bee so stout·
   And with so Clarkly cunning, their matter forge & fain,
   That certainely I can yeeld them equal paine.

But chiefly who be these (quod *Morpheus*) would I know
That thus above the rest, so cruelly bee used?
(Quoth hee) twoo Judges in Israell long agoe,
That sclandered *Susanna,* whome they would abused,

By fleshly deedes they thought to have misused,
  This vertuous wife and noble worthy Dame,
  Whom when she would not, accusde her with the same.

But bide a while (quoth hee) them selves shal make report,
And when thou hearest them, Judge as thou thinkest best:
And with these wordes out of that filthy sort,
With crooked hooke, hee halde them by the breast:
Whome when I vewed, with hande my selfe I blest.
  If I should tell of their deformed lookes,
  The rediest tongue, would fyre to reade the Bookes.

When up they cast their eyes, & *Morpheus* there behelde,
With woefulle looke, that ever eye did vewe:
For very sorrow with whorsy noise they yelde,
And crying sayde, oh happy dayes a dewe.
  Woe worth the daye alas, that Father us begot,
  And cursed bee our byrth, our mother slewe us not.[148]

Wee twoo in Israel whilome Judges were,
That al thing rulde among the Jewishe Nation:
In Babilon one *Joachim,* dwelling there,
And then among the Jewes in mighty estimation,
By meanes whereof to our contentation,
  No house so fitte as his, for us to lye and bee,
  Of whome againe no man more glad then hee.

Which *Joachim* one *Susanna* tooke to wife,
The onely Daughter of *Helchia* Just:
That lived chaste and vertuous all her life,
Who in the Lorde did ever put her trust:
Whose ardent beawty, styred up our lust

---

[148] Here is another example of Robinson's lack of consistency regarding the metre. There seems to be a line missing from the stanza but the MS is clear and this is correct.

So flamingly that like a gleyde wee broild,
This noble Dames chaste life to have defilde.

As in the thirteenth of *Daniel,* there it doth appeare,
What sleyght wee used burning in her love:
To come by cur purpose, wee brought her in dispayre,
For thus wee sweare by al the Gods above:
Except shee did consent that shee should hastely prove,
    For that wee had her there, we sayde wee would accuse her
    In filthy fornication we found aman abuse her.

Wee stealing in before the Orcharde doores were hard,
The rather then wee thought our purpose to have had:
But naked though shee stoode our talke shee not regarde,
O Lorde (quoth shee) nowe am I hard beestad:
Alas shee sayd, these ylles are bothe twoo bad.
    Yet had I rather byde these Tyrants accusation,
    Then for to yeelde and worke abhomination.

Which when we saw with open mouthes we cryed,
Fye upon this woman, an adulteresse (quod we)
At the which al the servauntes hasted fast and hyed,
And up they brake the doores, and in with speede they flee:
Wee accusing her, reported this wee see.
    Wherat the servants sad, made sorrow for the same,
    For why before, no man could staine her name.

Upon the morrowe before the elders all,
Wee falselye did accuse her there, upon the same:
But shee in prayer, upon her knees did fall,
And calde upon the Lord, in praysing of his name:
Whose eares heard wel her plaint: for shee from shame,
    By God delivered was: and wee to thraldome brought,
    The same wee had, as wee this Lady thought.

For by an Infauntes mouth, sturde up by God,
The verye truth of all our thoughtes revealde:

And in a worthy sentence, divulgate al abroade,
So that there was no Iote nor title once concealde:
And that wee both, sith then have sore bewailde.
    Daniel was his name, the Prophete of the Lord,
    That sav'de his servaunt, according to his worde.

And thus wee were reprooved of our false intent,
Susanna, set at libertye with joye and triple praise:
Daniel upon us, gave his cruel judgement,
Loe, thus at mischiefe ended wee our dayes:
The Gods condempne us, heare to lye alwayes.
    In paines perpetuall, whose endles woe no tongue
    Is able to describe, that wee have suffered long.

And world with worlds, withouten ende and ends,
Shall here bewaile our wilfull sclaunderous tongues:
And yet on earth are some that in the same offendes,
And thinke the Gods forget, because they suffer long:
(No no *Morpheus*) they doe revenge eache wrong.
    And sclaunder scapeth not, but heare is double quitte.
    Bee judge, that seest us thus formented in this pitte.

This odious vale throughout thou shalt not see,
The like to us, our plagues so faste increase:
Wishe al thy friendes therefore, like sclander for to flee,
For heare theyr paines loe, never have release.
Crye therfore betime, their tongues from sclander ceasse.
    He that from one or other theyr honest name doth take,
    Before the Gods a great offence doth make.

For wee unhappy wretches so much desired,
To have the use of this sayd noble Dame:
That like a gleide our inward sprites were fyred,
Our purpose to obtaine, wee forst no sinne nor shame:
But when wee were denied, wee falsely layde the blame
    Upon that vertuous wight, that never did offend,
    For our reward therefore behold the ende.

Some thinke theyr heeles be hoist, where head shall never come,
Whose eyes be bleard in glory vaine & balde,
And in theyr doultes conceyts, they thinke to geve yet dome,
Where they were never yet to counsel calde,
Whose purpose miste, theyr wilful blood doe scalde.
    Theyr Lordly heartes mand up with beggers purse,
    Doth worke the thing which afterward they curse.

But yet at mischiefe the sclandering tongue doth ende,
The proofe is plaine, if grace might guide the way:
The Gods doe still theyr servauntes true defende,
The wicked man doth ever lose his praye:
And in his pride comes sonest to decaye.
    Hee falleth through his owne imagination,
    As here by us the ende doth make probation.

O sclaunder, sclander, alas, woe worth the time,
That ever wee from hateful heart let flee:
By trifling tongue, those wicked dartes of thine,
To wounde theyr states that lived vertuouslye.
Take heede therefore al you that sclaunderers bee.
    Though our faulte therfore with you bee not regarded.
    Assure you yet, with us you are rewarded.

And with these wordes the cruell Jaylor straight,
With horrible gromeling noyse his trumpet soundes:
Where at like *Cadmus* seede they brawle and fight,
With crooked hookes eche one an other woundes.
To whome comes *Alecto* and scowling frownes,
    With greater plagues for to rewarde these lyers,
    And with hir breath settes all on flaming fiers.

Whereat I blest me to beholde their paines,
Ravisht of my witte almost, I went awaye.
Then when I thought how many here remaines,
Which practise nothing more then slaunder night & daye:
Thought I tis best from slaunder that you staye.

Accuse not true *Susanna,* the Lorde protects hir still,
His servaunt he defends and you shal want your will.

Away (quod *Morpheus*) I heare a mervels crye,
It seemes not farre, I wonder what it is:
With seeking up and downe, at length did there espie,
Another was rewarded for his wickednesse,
I long (quoth *Morpheus*) to know what noyse is this,
    And so we stayde, whereas we heard one saye,
    Lo wicked men your just rewarde for aye.

* * * * *

The Author to the two *Judges*

Whose tongue hath beene defylde with slaunders heretofore·
That humbly weepes not like a chyld, with great repeeting
    sore.
O wicked wretches fye, your Guerdon now is quit:
In *Tartarus* loe where you lie, that did in judgement sit.
Take heede you boasting blabbes, that Innocentes defyle:
You shall be whipt with cruell roddes, within this little while.
What sinfull deede is this, that woman to accuse,
That never yet was knowne amisse, hir body to abuse?
Howe dare you be so bolde, your neyghbors for to spoyle,
Of greater treasure then of golde, or fieldes of fertill soyle?
The mountes of *Mydas* pelfe, no crownes that Princes were:
Nor yet king *Alexanders* welth, to sell not halfe so deare
As is the honest name, whome evill tongues devoure,
Er now, that never yerned blame, are blotted in an houre.
But you that slaunderers bee, to minde *Susanna* call:
And prayse the Lorde, so shall you see Gods vengaunce on
    them fall·
For *Jacob* was accusde, poore man that thought none ill:
Alas how long hath spite bene usde, of them that want their
    will?
The slaundering tongue is such, if thought doe wag awry:
To winne the wager heele not grutche, thus to proclayme
    and cry:

That this or that I might, and will, and pleaseth mee:
And thou I ought to have of right, and sweres it so to bee.
Thus have I done sayth hee, when truth is nothing so:
Or else he sayth that this I see, to worke the parties wo.

And thus accused are, it pitieth me to heare,
Susannas that be guiltlesse, a thousande in a yeare.
Therefore you filthie Judges your ende I joye to see:
Now lye without refuge in Hell eternallie.
You sprang of *Cadmus* seede, your nature plaine doth sho:
But yet the Goddes at length doe weede, all such his
    servauntes fro.
With *Joachim* I doe rejoyce, *Susanna* thus to see
Elected by Goddes holie voyce, with Aungels for to bee.

Pope *Jhoan* rewarded for hir wickednesse[149]

The time that mortall men doe here abide,
Within this worlde that lasteth not an houre:
If fortune chaunce to smile upon their side,
Then still they strive from har to higher power.
    Content with present state not one there lives,
    But such as shoulde live best, the worst example gives.

Much woulde have more, the proverbe olde doth say,
Tis true indeede, much no man doth content:
For more and more all men doe gape eche daye,
They thinke the worlde will last and not be spent.
    Oh very fooles, deceyved foule ye bee:
    If happe be on your sides example take by mee.

To know my life, and what I was sometime,
Who lives and sees me lie amiddes this endelesse wo,
That woulde not doubt the like rewarde in fine,
That I deserved justly long ago?
    I must confesse my paine to little is,
    Though twentie times it were much worse then this.

Harke what I say the stoutst among you all,
Who fitteth hext that hath not cause to feare?
Some blast doth blow that gives the grievous fall,
Its often seene even once in twentie yere,
    Though Fortune hoyse the seates of some aloft,
    Yet shee delightes to cast them downe as ofte.

Nothing more brittle is then state of man,

---

[149] Robinson's account of this legendary popess probably comes from John Bale's *Pageant of Popes* (1555), translated into English by John Studley and printed again in 1574 (STC 1304). In the fourth book Bale mentions Joan as one of the examples of wickedness within the Catholic Church: 'Hytherto the Popes even to the forteth Pope cast theyr eyes on earthly things, forgetting Gods everlasting testament, as if they onely regarded but the fleshe, and not the soule [. . .] [Joan] sat as Pope in the pontificall seate at Rome two yeares, and syxe monethes' (Fol 55.105).

Both night and day experience doth appeere:
Yet notwithstanding, who doe not what they can,
To live like Goddes as long as they be heere?
    Though time do teache, al thinges begunne mast ende
    No mendement yet I see of such as doe offende.

Except the Gods they thought for to displace,
From out their seates wherein they sitte on hie:
Or that from *Jove* for to dispose the mace,
Wherewith hee rules the earth and all the skie:
    Else wot I not what all this mischiefe meanes,
    For *Codrus* lov'de of Gods, ritch men disdains.

On heapes to *Pluto* headlong here they runne,
Hell scarse is able the halfe part to holde:
The father is torment for wronging of his sonne,
And eke the sonne for like in triple folde.
    The mother for the daughter sustaines wo:
    The daughter for the mother, and many other mo.

But how happie be they that welth do not taste,
And that with povertie yelde thankes to the Gods?
No doubt above the starres all such men are plaste,
They be not scourged nor whipped with our roddes.
    Therefore by our harmes learne to be warned,
    Else shall you be sure with us to be charmed.

At the which wordes then *Morpheus* alofte did call,
What art thou (quod he) tell me thy name streight way?
(Shee aunswered) and sayde: even so with speede I shall,
If it please thee here a while to bide and stay.
    And if it be not long I am content (quoth he)
    And so with woful plainte these wordes declared she.

O *Morpheus Morpheus* I am that wofull wight,[150]
That once did sitte in *Peters* seate and place:
A man I seemde to be alas in all mens sight,
And yet a wicked woman the lesse my grace.
    I did take upon me the Gospell for to guide,
    Yet contrarie both I and mine did live besyde.

And *Jhoan* was I calde, and of my birth a Citie,
Named *Maience*[151] tooke hir proper name:
Brought up in learned scooles the more great pitie,
That grace had not beene lincked to the same.
    Learning I loved of all ritchesse under heaven,
    Till I conquered the knowledge of Sciences seaven.

I refused my countrie and frindes every one,
Many a Province I travaylde to and fro,
Better learned then my selfe I met not with one,
Of what estate or degree he were, high or loe.
    And in all these places where ever I came,
    I was thought among the people to be a very man.

In Englande once I was the countrey to peruse,
From thence to Roome I did returne with speede,
Within the which I did no deale refuse,
Gramer, Sophistry, Logike, and Rethorike, for to reade.
    My fellowe not founde, so ready was my braine,
    Nothing wanted *Morpheus,* but grace I tel thee plaine.

In *Lotaries* time, that Emperour was then,[152]
After the death of *Leo* by full election,

---

[150] Marginal Gloss: His words spoken to Morpheus.

[151] Modern day Menz (Mayence, Rhineland-Palatinate, Germany).

[152] Robinson refers to the emperor of Italy and later named a Carologian Emperor, who ruled over Nortern Italy, parts of German and parts of France, Lothair I (795–855AD). For a history see Heinrich Tiefenbach. *Studien zu Wörtern volkssprachiger Herkunft in karolingischen Königsurkunden: ein Beitrag zum Wortschatz der Diplome Lothars I. und Lothars II.* (W. Fink: München, 1973).

I was chosen for my wisedome aboue al men,
To have the Papall dignitye in my protection.
    And so was made Pope, and ruled as my lyst,
    Tyll my abhomination accusde mee or I wist.

For having at my wyll what harte could best thinke,
And ruling as it were all men as pleased mee:
Then layde I away both Booke, Pen, and Inke,
The swelling fleshe with them could not agree.
    I spared neyther Cardinal Bishop, Munke nor Frier,
    To fulfil my desire, I past not who they were.

Tyll at the last I chaunsed great with Childe,
At Saint *Johns Laterans* delivered was I:
And thus the Seate of *Peter* by mee was defilde,
Alas therefore full oft to late I crye.
    Afterwarde deposed I was, and so put downe,
    And begged my bread both in Countrey and Towne.

At this filthye acte the Gods were offended,
And sente mee to *Pluto,* his Judgement to trye:
Out of all the Heavens I was then suspended,
And heare am adlotted in paines still to lye,
    Loe, nowe thou knowest both the cause and my name,
    Therefore I pray thee warne thy friendes of the same.

Tell women, that have fine pollytike wittes,
That except they dread the Gods with honour due:
Whome Fortune hexte of all, with Scepture hits,
The hurtfull fall be they sure doth ensue.
    Although her nature bee sometime to smile,
    It's best yet take heede shee winke them not a wile.

From valley lowe, when Titan mounts the Hilles,
Hee doth dismount as fast as rise before:
The *Phoenix* scaling skies with singed quilles,
Turnes to the Earth againe, what needeth more?
    For fluddes that rise, when at the hexte they bee,
    Doe fall as fast againe, the proofe we see.

And finallye, will everye kinde of wight,
As well as women them selves, to knowe and see:
And that in time of wealth, they set theyr sight
To vewe what such doe wante that simpler bee.
    Their goodes and Landes with state of noble raine,
    Bewty, Youth, and al thinges els, shall shrinke againe.

You knowe the nine worthies lasted but a time,
The monstrous mountes do waste and weare awaye:
Then what is it that is made of sliche and slime,
That can upon the earth long stand or staye?
    All is but fleshe which wasteth like the snowe,
    When life shall part, the wisest doth not knowe.

Nowe alas, sith the world is thus unsure,
And fleshe so fraile, what fooles bee mortall men:
That have such hope in that for to endure,
That straight shall slip awaye they know not when?
    What gaines get they that winne a litle pelfe,
    For which the Gods at last condempne him selfe?

These wordes thus sayde, the rage of furious Hell,
With new invented miseries gan then to increase:
That very woe and sorrowe did compell,
This newe founde Pope from further talke to cease.
    Within my secreate hart, I pitied much her case,
    Bicause shee was a woman, and had so litle grace.

But then to see the great Souseheaded[153] Friars,
With Iommarnold Muncks, on heapes how fast they fel,
Beside platterfasde[154] Abbots, & Priests with pricke eares:

---

[153] As in the first *OED* definition: 1. a. Various parts of a pig or other animal, esp. the feet and ears, prepared or preserved for food by means of pickling.

[154] Platter-faced adj. having a face like a platter; also fig. 1533 Nicholas Udal, transl. Terence Floures for Latine Spekynge 199 b, That reed heeded, grey eyed, *plater-faced, and hawkenosed wenche. *OED*.

Howe busie they were it passeth tongue to tell.
   I thinke they sang for they gaped so wide,
   That to heare theyr service I might not abide.

Eache nowke was full of Nunnes, as busye as the best,
Properly apparelled like newe fashioned Players:
Prating Pardoners, were Cookes of the Feast,
Whose scullions were a number of beastly Southsaiers.
   Every one occupied, not one of them was idle,
   But neyther with Testament nor with Sacred Bible.

At length they fell out what so ever was the matter,
They fought with Sensars, and holy water Cans:
Great Beades about eache others face they clatter,
I litle thought they had beene such men of theyr hands.
   We saw them so disquiet, we stoode from them afarre,
   For feare of blowes before that wee were warre.

I sawe no man there that seemde to make peace,
The like maistries at *Olimpus,* were never so made:
Thicke and threefold on heapes they lye like Beastes,
Theyr nayles were so long no man calde for a blade.
   Thus violently they disguised one of them the other,
   In such fury, that the son tormented his owne Mother.

It was a wonder to mee verye straunge,
To see what May games they made in that pitte:
Like Maisters of Fence (great stroakes they did chaunge
One with another) starke madde out of witte.
   A marvailous Musicke, a prayer most painfull,
   Among Christian people nothing more dainfull.

Whereat (quod *Morpheus*) looking on mee,
Doest thou behold (quoth hee) what miserye is here,
And what presumption in some women may bee,
And howe to come by theyr purpose, full litle they feare·
   But what mischiefe is this, heare for to finde,
   These Popes & these prelates ye to preach were assinde?

These are they which beare the world in hand,
That in heaven and Hell, they had evermore power:
(As they sayde) so it was, and with God did stande,
Out of Hell to fetche thousandes of soules in one hower.
    And no worde true all was fables and lyes.
    With false Doctrine and Idolatry the bleard our eyes.

These are the Bellye Gods,[155] that outward did appeare,
To bee most holye, and just alway in theyr living:
Which before God very Hipocrites were,
And liv'de like brute Beasts, without any thanks geving.
    They pleade a Priviledge, to doe what theyr lyst,
    As if Hell and Heaven were both in theyr fist.

And thus wee departed and left the new found Pope,
With her College of Cardinals, and other her mates:
At hext of theyr service without vestment or Cope,
With nailes large and long, they bispte each others pates.
    So downe the dales, wee drewe to beholde,
    The manifold mischiefe among yong and olde.

Whome then to see through many a knaggy crust,
And brethles blast, with stormes as Kasor kene:
And scaping dartes all redde with cankred rust,
Wee passed through, of any one not seene.
    Yet by the way a thousand sightes we see,
    Of which to thinke, full ofte it greeveth mee.

Tyll at the laste, wee drewe unto the place,
And hurtfull hole in cruell *Stigion* lake:
Whereas wee heard a man bewaile his case.
No pained soule, might greater sorrow make.

---

[155] A Belly-God, according to the *OED*, is 'One who makes a god of his belly; a glutton' and has been in use in English since 1540.

These wordes me thought, the wofull wretch did crye,
Come see (alas alas) the tormentes where wee lye.

The torment of Tiranny, and the reward for his wickednesse; Being a King called *Mydas*: which Tirannouslye, swallowed not onely his Countrey for Lucre sake, but his householde Servauntes also[156]

Thus as wee left these Romish Roges, of whome I spake of late,
Wee chaunste to heare a woeful wight, yet did bewaile his state.
And *Tiranny* his name was calde, who lov'd to leime[157] the poore,
And suppe the gaine of sweating browes, for to increase his store.
This mighty mate ne mercy mindes, when he on soile did dwell,
But eate up all on every side, as they that want can tel.
The widow and the Fatherles, the Stranger that doth toyle:
His household Servitours and al, hee seeketh for to spoyle.
Whome lended hee his eares unto, but onelye unto suche,
As unto *Pluto* sacrifizde theyr soules to gaine him muche?
Tyl at the last his Tiranny, the ayre corrupt with smell,
Whereat the Skies, did turne theyr hewe, and *Limbo* gan to yell.
The Mountaines roare by *Eccos* voice, into the Heavens hye,
The scrikes and cryes of wronged wights, and al togeather flye.
The Preachers powred teares apace, repentance styl they cryde,
But al in vaine, his eares were stopte, such newes he might not bide.
His stoared ground, his racked rents, his heards of goats, with sheepe &

---

[156] Robinson combines the stories of the legendary and the historical Midas: The legendary king of Phrygia, famous for his golden touch and his ass's ears (made notable in Ovid's *Metamorphoses*). The historical king of Phrygia (738-696 BCE) was the first barbarian king to offer gifts to the oracle at Delphi (*OCD*). His primary source materials for this is probably Golding's Ovid.

[157] Lieme: 'Light, flame; a flash, ray, or gleam of light; brightness, gleam. Also fig. Forms: 1 leoma, 2 lome, 3-4 leome, lem, 3-6 (9) leme, (4 leom, lewme, lime, lym, Sc. leyme), 4-5 leem, (5 leeme, Sc. leime), 4, 6-7 leame, 6- leam. [OE. leoma str. masc. = OS. liomo, ON. lióme: OTeut. *leuhmon-, f. *OED*.

His prowling pickthanks, made him to forget his duty
   cleane:
Whom when yet *Jove* perusde, and searchte his flintish
   Pharaos heart, graine,
Upon the snappe grimme *Mors* he sends, to stick him with
   his Dart.
Who wound him so, that *Atropos* to line straight laid the
   launce,
Gods people by this Tyrants death, from bondage to
   advaunce.
Whose wandring ghost, to *Charons* bote, with fearful grenes
   is gone,
To dwell among the damned sprites, for other hope is none:
Where, in a pit, a place is pitchte, a woeful chayre to sit,
In molten mettall to the Crowne, a place for Tyrantes fit.
His officers bande him round about, with bagges of money
   thrust,
Which never cease, with gnashing teeth, to lend him many a
   dust.
Medusa is his Cook, to dresse this wretche his meate,
Which sets before him crawling Snakes, and ugly Todes to
   eate.
His counsellers bee retcht on length, theyr Guts on hookes
   bee torne,
Whose fowle deformed filthy tongus bewaile that they were
   borne·
Thus tost & torne, with torments great, with thunderbolts
   bethwakt,
On forkes & fleshhooks streind & stretcht, eche ioynt from
   other crakt,
And to augment this Misers griefe, with hookes they hale
   him out
Uppon a frosen scaffolde hoyst, this Tyraunt lookes about:
Where Hellish Hegges and Furies shewe a sight t'increase
   his paine
Which is the joyfull *Eden* fieldes, where saved soules
   remaine.
The blisfull bankes there might he see, the valleyes sweete &
   fayre,

Where wants no floures of noble taste, for to perfume the ayre.
All kinde of fruites do shew themselves, and readie ripe they hynge,
Of pleasures passing man to wishe, there wantes no kinde of thinge·
Pernassus hill to base a bancke, to be comparde to this,
Or *Helicon* in such respect, a weedie pyngle is.[158]
Nor *Cithera* pearle of all the earth, is ought but counterfet,
Though it were deckt with all the golde, that *Alexander* get
Tho I had dronke and supped up, sweete *Aganippes* well,
Or *Gabanelus* skilfull floodes, yet want I skill to tell
The heapes of joyes, this joyfull fielde is garnished with all,
Doth much surmount this worldly blisse, thrise more then suger gall
For there Sir *Tellus* doth not taste of *Hiemps* frosen face,
Nor *Boreas* bragges the weakest twigge, sturs not within that place·
For *Phebus* hee his golden beames, disperseth here and there:
And *Jupiter* the silver droppes from skies doth cause retire.
(In *season* due) to molifie these fieldes of endelesse blisse,
Where none may come but such as by the Goddes appoynted is.
Whose garmentes be as white as snow, on instrumentes they sing.
And never cease, but praysing God, of earth, and heaven king.
And crownes upon their heads they were, & aungels foode they eate,
Still *Gloria in excelsis* sing to th' Lambe upon the seate.
There might this Tyraunt well beholde the poore whome he oprest·
Amid these joyes for evermore, appoynted for to rest.

---

[158] Pyngle: A fierce contest or fight; contention, open disagreement. Obs.: 1543 *St. Papers Hen. VIII V*. 237 (note) [They made at each other, so that] with long pyngle with dagger [Somerset was slain] *OED*.

And such as least he did esteeme, and all be rent with wrong,
Their happie life eche houre did see, and daylie hearde their song.
Which when he hearde, a triple paine assaultes this caytives ghost.
When hee did way his mundane mucke, and heavens treasure lost:
In equall ballaunce when he tryed, how Conscience him accusde,
(Quoth hee) fie on you Impes of Hell, that thus have me abusde.
Meaning by the muckhill Mates, which whispred in his eare,
And taught him how Goddes people poore, for gaines to rend & teare.
To ride, to runne, to hale, and drawe, as bondeslaves every houre,
To whippe and scourge no mo then all, that were within his poure.
But Oh (quoth hee) let all the worlde example take by mee,
Let never greatest Prince on earth thinke other but to dye.
Oh, fye on goodes, thryse fye on golde, and tentimes fie on such
As shall procure great mightie men, the poore by wrong to touch.
And then he wrange his handes for wo, what happe had I (quoth hee)
To lende my eares to Dunghil Doltes[159], at their commaunde to bee,
And banisht from my service quite, the bloode of gentle race,
Which alwayes counsaylde me to minde, mine honor and my grace?

---

[159] Dolt: [Found with its derivatives from middle of 16thc.; perh. earlier in dialect use. App. related to OE. dol, ME. dol, doll, Dull, and to DOLD, stupid, inert of intellect or faculty. For the -t, cf. ME. dult in sense of dulled:]. A dull, stupid fellow; a blockhead, numskull. *OED*.

But as the Ravens seeke their praye, or Woolfe the spoyle
    pursues,
So did the Churles by meanes of me, eache where their furie
    use.
The sonnes of Theeves & rustick Carles, might leade me as
    they list,
So that the gobs of gloring golde, they brought to freight my
    fist.
Yet as they spoylde the coast abroade (from me) so did they
    pinche,
So that at everye elne, I scarce receyved halfe an inche.
I pitied not the Wydowes cause, nor fatherlesse I wayde,
Both townes and countries rounde about, to pastures great I
    layde·
Yet had I mines, with vineyardes large, with corne and
    cattell store
Yea Lordships, lands, parckes houge & wide, yet stil I lookt
    for more.
Mules and Camels infinite, Townes and Castles greate,
Thus *Fortune* with hir smiling lookes, hir worldly hookes can
    bayte
To catche the covetous Tyrant with, to present to *Plutos*
    grace,
Whose wickednesse he doth rewarde full well within this
    place.
And then hee lookt upon these slaves, much yll (quoth he)
    betide,
You herlots borne, that thus bewitcht a Prince of such a
    pride
Much yll and wo may hap to thee, thou foule deformed
    slave.
And all thy mates that mooved mee, this mundan mucke to
    crave.
The childe unborne curse you & yours, the hils shall sounde
    the same,
The stones in streets cry out on you, the skies proclaime
    your shame.
The heavens abhor both you and yours: Hell rend you with
    his jawes,

And Furies all in *Stigion* streames, torment you with their
    clawes·
Much more he sayde but what it was, for skrikes we coulde
    not tell,
His men of trust and hee that time, in tormentes so did yell.
But still they bang him with these bagges, like madmen in
    their rage
And streite these furies with their hookes, did mount him
    from the stage.
Where tumbling hee in molten golde, doth walter here and
    there,
Till at the length, of him nor his, we coulde not see nor here.
But over the pit with letters blacke, this sentence there was
    pende
This is the place of just rewarde for Tyrauntes in the ende.
Then by and by, a thundring voyce came poudering up the
    pitte,
(Which sayde) *remember thende you men, in chayres of state*
    that sit.
For Pluto is the Jaylor here, to mightie Jove above:
He pardons none but all alike, (take heede it doth behoove)
Which words did make my hart to shrink, as flowers doe in
    June,
So that to speake one worde for life, I durst not once
    presume.
But in my heart I wisht all men, King *Mydas* mucke to flee,
And speciallye the number that of mightie honor bee.
For they that reade the Poetes workes, shal here of *Mydas*
    much,
And how he crav'de all to be golde that he might feele or
    touche.
But though the Poets fabled so, and I in dreames doe faine,
Yet let not Tyrauntes better trust, but taste of *Plutos* paine.

RICHARD ROBINSON

The rewarde that *Rosamond* had in Hell, for murdering of hir husbande *Albonius* and living vitiouslie in hir husbandes dayes[160]

When from this Pope we were depart and gone,
Meaning to returne, the night was almost spent:
But there fast by we hearde one crye anon,
Which sayde (Alas, alas) to late I doe repent,
    My wanton dayes, my lustie youthfull toyes,
    Have banisht me from Aungels part of joyes.

The sounde there of a woman did present,
For Screminglie it rang among the caves,
Which when we hearde we coulde not be content:
But scalde the cragges among the flaming waves.
    Till at the last a dungeon had we spyde,
    Wherein the woman was that latelye cryde.

And as we stoode thereof to take the vewe,
In scalding furnesse whose flash doth still increase,
A seeming noble Dame with crowne and sceptare newe
(Among a number) gan first of all to prease,
    And sayd (Oh *Morpheus*) such haste why dost thou make·
    I pray thee bide a while, yet for a womans sake.

Wherefore (quoth hee) my presence doth no good,
And yll I may abide, the night is almost spent:
Shee hearing this, cryed out as one were wood,
Abide and beare two wordes, then go I am content.

---

[160] Robinson's account of Rosamond probably comes from Lydgate's *Fall of Princes*. Boccaccio, Lydgate's source, included details of how Rosamond was unfortunate in life but then murdered her husband Alboyus so that she could live with her lover Melchis. They escape to Ravenna and marry. Eventually Rosamond falls in love with the governor of Ravenna and decides to kill Melchis. He, however, learns of her deceit and makes her partake of the same poison he drinks (STC 3175).

Dispatche (quoth hee) for long I cannot bide,
But first of all, thy name and cause describe.

(Oh quoth shee) this place prepared is,
For wickednesse the just rewarde to bee,
And such as live against the Goddes amisse,
Be used here with tormentes as you see.
 Sith *Morpheus* thou all dreames dost shew eche where,
 Publish this abroade how we are used here.

And let them know how *Rosamonde* the Queene,
To *Albonyus* late wife that was sometime,
Lyeth torment here as thou hast present seene,
For filthie life, and odious bloodie crime.
 My life did crave none other ende but this,
 Therefore beholde rewarde of wickednesse.

Therefore let mee to women warning bee,
To honor God the beste, and next their spoused mates:
And say that *Rosamonde* thus sayde to thee,
Who doth not so, shall enter at these gates.
 It doth become eache woman night and daye,
 To holde them well content, at what their husbandes saye,

You lustie bloodes possest with hawtie hartes·
Your loftie lookes correct with meaner state,
Refuse to playe these wanton wilfull partes,
From follye flee, least you repent to late.
 Sometime I lookte as hye as hexte of you,
 Which is the onelye cause I bid al joyes adewe.

Seeme not to swell a hast ye worde to heare,
No vauntage seeke, nor quarrels frame to breede:
An honest womans part is ever to forbeare
The sayinges of her husband, if wel shee thinke to speede.
 Where love is linkte, wordes cannot brewe the bate,
 But where dissemblers are, fewe wordes then causeth hate.

And laye aside your newe disguised raye,
Leave prancking of your selves with painted face:
From whirling heyre and there your eyes prophaned stay,
Bee faithful Matrons found in every place.
    Who doth hir spowsed Mate in any case betraye,
    Shall sure repent it sore, with mee another daye.

For if that grace had light upon my side,
Then had I dread before the doubtfull ende:
And so escaped that which nowe alas I bide,
As Guerdon meete for them that so offend.
    For through one word I heard my husband saye,
    My stomack was so stowte, I made him straight away.

Which was but small and easie to bee borne,
But that the wicked sprite mee tempte to seeke his blood,
For even as Judas his Maisters death had sworne,
Infect with like temptacion, that present time I stoode.
    Vengeance I invented, and vengeance have I caught·
    To seeke my Husbandes life, mine owne destruction brought.

Loe, this was the cause: At my Husbands returne,
From doing great Battailes in Countreys full farre:
Being his pleasure a while for to Sojourne,
To rest him at ease after his Warre:
    Let call a Triumphe, and made a great Feast,
    To the which assembled all his Lordes of the best.

And being in his meriment, thus Jested with mee:
Tooke a Goblet with Wine, and these words then he sayd:
(Drinke a tawnt to thy Father, Wife quoth hee)
Who before in Battaile was wounded to dead.
    Thus for to saye, much is not a mis,
    Who ever doth speake it, where any grace is.

But (alas) unhappilye I, as most women bee,
Was pufte full of Pride, and mutable minde:
I swelde as a Toade his death for to see,

Yet spake I him fayre his sences to blinde:
   O God what mischiefe can women invent,
   And if a man alter but once theyr intent.

When I spake him as fayre as heart might devise,
And made the greatst shewe of Faithfull true love:
Inwardlye then I dyd hate and despise,
My noble Husbande all Creatures above.
   Therefore I confesse, it is harde for to knowe,
   When a woman speakes fayre, if shee meanes it or no.

I polluted filthilye my Husbandes bedde,
With one of his servauntes, whome after I made
Most Traiterously to smite of his head,
As hee laye a sleepe with his owne sworde or blade.
   And so tooke his Treasure, and to the Seas wee fled,
   There leaving my Husband wounded to dead.

This Squiers name, that did this wicked deede,
Melchis was called a stoute worthy Knight:
In *Ravenne* there became to proceede
A mighty Prince of great power and might.
   Yet for all this, with him straight I tyred,
   For eache daye on my filthy lust beastly desired.

Were hee Gentle or simple, I spared none,
Of one above another, I made no store:
For shame, Feare, and Grace, from mee were quite gone,
I paste not a pinne were they Ritche or poore:
   My filthy fleshe so wickedly was sette,
   That all was but fishe that came to the nette.

But among al the rest one noble man,
That then of *Ravenne* was a governour:
As ofte as pleased him nowe and than,
Had greate delite to holde mee as Paramour.
   On whome a while my flitting minde did runne,
   As erst it had of *Melchis* latelye done.

For whose sake *Melchis* my husbande newe,
Through treason framde, and vile Duplicitye,
Within my heart his death, I gan to brewe,
Because at large I thought to live more viciously.
    To worke the feate by sleyght, and scape the blame,
    I privily poysoned wine, & made him drinke the same.

To the middes dranke *Melchis* this Cup of Wine,
Which made him looke with colour dead and wan:
But when hee sawe that Traytresse heart of mine,
With much a doe these wordes declare hee gan
    With rufull face. Thou wicked wretche (quoth hee)
    Albonius thou through Treason slew, so hast done me.

And there withall his hande uppon mee layde,
And urged me in Maugre of my head,
To drinke the tother halfe before I staide,
Which was no soner done but downe wee both fell dead,
    And thus at mischiefe ended I my life,
    That sometime was a Famous Princes Wife.

Loe *Morpheus,* this is the summe and all:
Nowe thou knowest my name, my wicked fact and deede:
I praye thee yet what haste soever fall,
Warne women of the like, it's not a litle neede.
    To theyr Spowsed mates, bid them bee meeke & true,
    Or tell them else confution doth ensue.

Bid them meeken theyr mindes with al due obedience,
And to humble them selves to theyr Husbandes alwayes:
For it is commonlye seene by auncient experience,
That none but the wilful doe catche their decaies.
    Though wylye in working the craftie Dames bee,
    Them selves they deceave in the ende you may see.

And now farewel *Morpheus* thou wotes what I meane,
Thou mayest say thou met with a *miserable* wight:
That first procured her Husband to bee slaine,
And also poysoned a valiaunt Knight.

This was my acte and the cause of my fall,
Quite murther, for murther, my selfe laste of all.

And with these wordes a Tyraunt with a hooke,
In tender sides, the mortall woundes hee printes,
Another on a forke this wicked woman shooke,
Nothing prevailed lesse, then for to crye with plaintes
    A thousande naked blades in her they thrust,
    And still (quoth they) this woman was unjust.

Mee thought it was a feareful sight to see,
Pitye wrought such griefe in mee, I wept for woe:
I thought that in a womans heart, had layen more pitye,
Then for to serve her faithfull Husband so.
    Why dost thou muse (quoth *Morpheus*) then to mee?
    This is the just reward of them that wicked bee.

The night is almost spent (quoth hee) come let us goe,
The least of theyr paines passeth our helpe:
I will bring thee safe to the place thou came fro,
Bee not doubtful of *Cerberus* that fowle currishe whelpe,
    Nor of any that is heare, I will answere them all:
    Bee of good cheere what ever doe be fall.

Thus wandering backe, wee looked about,
And or ever wee wist, were at *Plutoes* Pallaice:
At the which wee heard so cruell a showte,
As if they had all gon togither in malice,
    Yet when we came neere them the truth then appeered,
    It was but a triumph, and nought to be feared.

Then after a while upon a stage full hye,
An yll faste yoman a blacke Trumpet blew:
And when silence was made, hee proclaymed a crye,
In the name of *Pluto* for tydinges most true.
    (Quoth hee) bloodie *Boner* the Butcher comes here,
    That hath furnisht our kitchin this many a yere.

Moreover (quoth hee) it is *Plutos* high pleasure,
That all men prepare in the best sort they can,
Sith he is to *Pluto* and *Proserpin* such treasure,
To receyve him amonge us as becomes such a man,
    You know what his service hath bene heretofore,
    Looke to your dueties what needes any more?

This sayde, he departed straite from the stage,
And to *Plutos* Pallace hee then tooke the waye.
But then to see both man boye and Page,
To set newe deventions in order and raye,
    The halfe to declare, it passeth my witte,
    I am sure the like, was never seene yet.

There was fyling of fire boltes in holes and in noukes,
Headding of dartes, and poynting of spittes,
Skouring of blades, and bending of hookes,
Mending of fireforkes, and wyring newe whipes,
    Barreling of Pitche, Sulfur, and Saltepeeter,
    With more then can be described in meeter.

But for to be briefe so willing they were,
That nothing was wanting to set out the showe,
As by their dilligence full well did appeere,
No man coulde be more welcome there I know.
    Boner (quoth one) *Boner* quoth another,
    Welcome as hartelye as Father or Mother.

With all thinges poynt vice, and fit for the nonce,
Foorth came *Pluto,* and *Proserpin* the Queene,
To meete *Boner* the sucker of soules, flesh, and bones,
In such order and sorte as hath not bene seene.
    I shall make a description as nie as I can,
    How they went in order to meete him eche man.

First two and two came marching togither,
With a Pickeforke or Fleshooke in every fist,
A blacke banner displayed that wavered in the weather,
Which obscured the light with darcke stinking mist.

Yll faste Trumpiters a number there were,
From whose mouthes flewe a thunder odible to here.

The number I knew not so many there were,
But brave and fine they were out of doubt:
In hattes like hives, and hoase bumde with heare
With rough courlde heades, they looked full stout,
    They were so lustie they seemde to be cutters,
    For they made it tentimes as bigge as swarfe Rutters.[161]

Next after these there came in a raye,
By heapes whole swarmes of *Plutos* nobilitie,
Which did ride upon Beares that did gape for their praye,
That alwayes were fed with the spoyle of simplicitie,
    About their neckes hang double chaynes of golde·
    But to aske their names I durst not be bolde.

Then came his Chapleins by two and by three,
And after them followed the great Vicare of all,
And on his heade a triple Crowne ware hee,
Arayed in robes that were full Pontificall,
    On a ramping Lyon that gaped full wide,
    This greasie Prelate that present did ride.

And then followed *Pluto* and *Proserpin* his Queene,
Upon as straunge horses as ever I see,
For like the hote gleydes glowed their eine,
Mightie and monstrous, long, large, and hie
    With a number of Lordes, and Ladies also,
    Came after in order, beside other moe.

Cerberus was taught in the Porters warde,
The gutes were set open against *Boner* came,
Of *Morpheus,* and mee no man tooke regarde,
Their minde ranne so much of this noble man.

---

[161] i.e. Swooning calvary (cf. OED swarfe; rutter).

By meanes whereof without more a doe,
We gate out o'th gates or any man knewe.

Being out of the gates we scaled a rocke,
To see if wee might there spie *Boner* comming,
Who in deede appeared in sight with a flocke,
That came like Bedlems hedlong then running.
    Himselfe led the way like a Champion stoute,
    On a Dragons backe that spoylde rounde aboute.

He kept no order nor the companie that he brought,
For headelong came reeling both olde and young,
As thicke as haylestones, a man woulde have thought,
Whereof some cryed, and othersome soung.
    But downe the hyll one and other came tumbling,
    With *Sancta Maria,* I hearde them fast mumbling.

A banner was borne with red all to spotted,
Before this butcher that pittie was to see,
Whose armes in the middes was rufully blotted,
With the bloode of Martyres whome he caused to die.
    And in the shielde painted as plaine did appeere,
    An innocent Lambe, a cruell Woolfe, and a Beare.

In a fielde all blacke, on the other side his flagge,
Was depainted a fagot that glowed like a gleede,
And a bluddie hande with a sworde that did bragge,
Gainst all that profest Christes Gospell in deede.
    With a poasie that threatned both aged and young,
    To be leeve in his lore, or else howe their tongue.

But then to see what a meeting there was,
Betweene *Pluto, Proserpin,* and *Boner* that time,
For want of skill I must let it passe,
I cannot mention th'one halfe in this rime.
    (No displeasure to the *Pope*) if himselfe had bene there,
    It had not beene possible to made him better cheare.

Mary what they sayd, that, wee did not know,
But there was for joye such colling and kissing:
Some laught that teeth a foote long they did show,
And clawde eache other by the pate without missing.
    To see the triumph made with fleshhookes & spits,
    Had bene able to have brought a man from his wits.

For thunder and lightning flew fizing about.
Dartes and firebrandes walkt here and there,
Bonfiers were made in all Hell throughout,
For joye that *Boner* was comming so neere.
    Whose face I frayde least he shoulde have spide me,
    For when he was living he might not abide me.

Behinde *Morpheus* I crept, till they marched by,
And were past as farre as *Cerberus* warde,
But when they were within we hearde such a crye,
As among all the sorrowes before I not hearde.
    They set bell on fire with making a feast,
    And all was to welcome this lately come gest.

What was *Boners* Businesse that I doe not knows·
Peradventure he went to fetche soules away thence.
But judge as you list therein yea or no,
I would not be with him for all the Popes pence.
    But if Boners babes doe thinke that I lie,
    Then let them go thither the truth for to trie.

The ende of *The Rewarde of Wickednesse*

RICHARD ROBINSON

Retourning from Plutos Kingdome, To Noble Helicon: The place of Infinite Joye.

When wee from *Plutos* Pallaice came, and vewed had this woe.
(Quod *Morpheus*) yet I have a walke, a litle waye to goe.
For sith I have take al this paine, the doleful place to see,
My friendes shall knowe of my affayres, for that I am so nye.
This viage hight I long a goe, performde my promise is,
As thou thy selfe who eare demaunde, shal witnesse bee of this.
My Ladies lookte for mee long since, some uncouth newes to heare.
And howe in *Stigion* flames they sped, that living, wicked were.
Therefore it standes mee much upon, my promise to performe,
For that unto these worthy Dames, so firmely I have sworne.
It nothing doth behove (quoth hee) with them to bawke or blooke,
For why they doe from mighty Gods, descende of Sacred stocke.
Of *Mercurie* the onely sayde *Minervas* dearlinges deere,
Whose mightie Muse, and learned skill, had never yet theyr peere.
In *Helicon* their dwelling is, with *Cytheron* full hye,
Pernassus for theyr pleasure have, when they thereto agree.
And loe, where (*Helicon*) appeares of truth a princely place,
Where thou and I, these Ladies with, must commen face to face.
At which mine eyes I lifted up: The fore sayde place I see,
Which was mee thought so passing fine, as never thing might bee.
The Redrose, and the Rosemarye, Invironed this Hill,
In everye nooke the Gilyflower, him selfe presented styll.
The comely Bancks with Daysies deckt, and Primrose out of crie,
The Violets and Cowleslops sweete, abought in sight I spye.

With other Hearbes that pleasaunt were, which did mee
    good to see.
Whose fragrant smels perfume the ayre, yet from this place
    doth flee,
The Thrustel and the Nightingale, with Musike sweete they
    Pipe,
So pleasauntlye the Gods them selves to heare would much
    delite.
Loe, here doe yeeld the Christal Springs, theyr trickling
    silver floods,
And there Pomgarnet Tree with fruite, to earth doth veile his
    buds.
The Filbeard in another place, as browne as Beryes shoe,
Elfstones I spyed the Orrange hyng, with Quince and many
    moe.
What wast that wanted there (nothing) that might delite the
    minde·
But hee that lookte (in every place) the same should present
    finde.
In triple wise the Arbours cast, I made of sweetest Briar,
Mirt with the Vine, that up and downe the ripest grape doth
    beare.
Of Bore are Turrets dubbed round, & stayres by arte wel
    wrought
Tascende into the tops thereof, as fine as maye bee thought.
Wherein these Ladies ofte doe sit, this Joyfull sight to vewe,
For there they maye afarre, beholde what strangers come a
    newe.
And when wee had perusde this place, of highe and mightye
    fame,
In hexte of al these Turret tops, wee spied a noble Dame,
Adornde and deckte, in comelye raye, and seemely to
    beholde,
Hir face was like an Angel bright, whose hayre that steinde
    the gold.
Not curld and fruzulde her browes about, but combde in
    order fayre,
And on her head of Laurell made, a garlande which shee
    ware.

No double Ruffes about her necke, no garded Gowne ware
    shee,
Nor on her handes that steinde the snow, no ringes there
    were to see.
Hir eyes stoode stedfast in her head, they whirlde not here
    and there·
Nor in her face you could espye, ought else but grace
    appeare.
A comely Gowne shee had upon, of collour sad and sage,
As best became a worthy Dame, presenting midle age.
To whome wee drewe in al the haste, our reverence for to
    use,
Whom when shee saw, first word shee said, welcome (quoth
    she) what newes·
But further or I do proceede, her name I shal describe,
And in what order that I see, hir Sisters in that tide.
Melpomina, this Ladye hight, the eldest of the nine,
That there among hir Sisters sate, within that Turret greene.
And everye Ladye with a Booke, in studie sate full fast,
And reading of the worthy actes, that had beene done and
    past.
The workes of Poets all they had, and scanning there they
    were·
Who was best worthy in his time, a Poets name to beare.
And Instruments in every nowke, these noble Ladies had,
To recreate theyr Muses with, and for to make them glad.
And everye one appareyld like, whose face like starres did
    shine,
Respondent to *Melpomina,* In gracious giftes divine.
Among them were no wanton songs, nor *Bacchus* banequets
    sought
Nor newe device of prancking Pride, nor signe of evill
    thought.
There was no care to purchase lande, nor fleessing of the
    poore,
Nor renting Houses out of crye, nor hording for a store.

There was no Striving for such pelfe, as worldlinges nowe
    delite,

Tom Teltale could not there bee found, that worketh al the spite.
Nor *Peter Pickthancke* beare no swaye, for all his craftye fatche,
The Bailife *Laurence Lurcher,* there hath nothing for to catche.
There is no Tyrant there, that spoiles nor doth yet poore man wrong,
No taking in of Commons is, within that circuite long.
One seekes not there anothers blood, his livinges to obtaine,
No privie hate, nor open wrath, among them doth remaine.
Hipocrisie doth take no place, among these worthye Dames,
Of any Crime it is not heard, that one another blames.
The ruggie blast of *Boreas* mouth, at no time taketh place,
There *Ver,*[162] and *Flora,* both do shewe theyr gorgious face.
Nor *Zephirus* doth shake no braunche, within that sacred Hill,
But every thing in former state, alwayes continueth styll.
Nor *Hiemps* hath no power there, the flakye Snowe to cast,
There is nothing that taketh taste, of cruell Winters blast.
And as I sayde ere while, hawe that wee did these Ladies spie,
(So what wee sayd) and they to us, Ile tell you by and by.
When wee in order found them thus: Haile Ladye *Morpheus* sayde,
With Cap in hande I vailde to earth: (They bad mee hele my heade)
(And welcom *Morpheus*) one and all, they sayde rejoysinglie,
Why hast thou bene so long (quod they) what newes hast brought with thee·
What newes (quod *Morphe*) newes enough, aread from whence I came

---

[162] This is the personified springtime. E.g. : 1390 Gower, *Conf.* III. 118 Whan Ver his Seson hath begonne. c1400 *Destr. Troy* 4037 Ver entrid full euyn, eger with all. 1430-40 Lydagte's *Bochas* V. xv. (1554) 132 Ver came in with hys newe grene. a1547, Surrey in *Tottel's Misc.* (Arb.) 8 There might I se how Ver had euery blossom hent. 1568 T. Howell's *Arb. Amitie* (1879) 24 Now Lady Ver in lively greene doth showe her grace in fielde. *OED.* Flora is, of course, the goddess of Flowers in Latin mythology.

I have performde my promise made, as ought an honest
    man.
You did request and I agreede to vewe vile *Stigion* lakes,
And to peruse with wicked sorte, what order *Pluto* takes.
And how they are rewarded there, it was your willes to
    know,
That did delite in evill actes to worke poore people woe.
(Quoth they thats true) & were you there? I came from
    thence (quod hee)
Then all at once they gave him thankes, as glad as they
    might bee.
With modest words tell us (quod they) what sightes that you
    have seene
For thankes is all you get of us, to quite your toyled paine.
But what we can or may be boulde, that honest seemes to
    bee,
(To pleasure you) in any wise, we shall thereto agree.
But speake, tell on, lets lose no time (quoth one) we thinke it
    long,
Begin good *Morpheus* (quoth the rest) and we will holde our
    tongue.
So *Morpheus* streight began his tale, and toulde them how
    that hee·
Among a Masque of merye mates, by chaunce did light on
    mee.
And howe wee past from ward to ward, & what was done
    and sayde,
And when wee came to *Plutoes* place, among them howe wee
    sped.
And whome we saw, and what they did, & what theyr
    sayinges was,
Correspondent to the trueth discribed, more and les.
But when hee tolde them of the Pope, that *Alexander* hight,
And of the Service that they sang, and used day and night:

And what resort of Shavelings hee, had with him every
    howre,
The Ladyes all on Laughing fell, yea, rounde about the
    Tower.

Yet wofull for the rest they were, because they wanted grace,
For very zeale these worthy Dames, in teares did washe theyr face.
Where at when *Morpheus* did behold, these Ladies woful cheare,
(Quod hee) if I had thought on this, I would not have come heare.
But cease your dolour yet a while, your listning eares lende mee,
And wipe away those plainting teares, which greeveth me to see.
For certs I have, of woefuluesse and dyrefull destnye tolde,
Of pleasaunt Pageantes Ile rehearse, & Triumphs many folde.
In wandring up and downe the vale, to see these uglye fightes,
About the place where *Pluto* laye, wee sawe great Lampes & lights.
With Pageands playd, and Tragedies, & noise of Trumpets sound,
Yea, Bonfires blasde, with thumping guns, that shooke the trembling ground.
Which when we hard, & did behold, we hasted fast to know,
What was the cause, wherfore or why, those trumpets gan to blow.
And comming to the Pallaice Gates, wee neede not crave them why,
For *Boner* comes with open Jawe, both yong and olde gan crye.
So *Morpheus* set the Tale an ende· and as I sayde of late,
One so as *Boner* welcomde was, at large discride the state.
Where at the Ladies every one, with comely smiling cheare,
Laide by their Bookes, & laught ful fast, those newes of him to heare
Aha (quoth they) is *Boner* there? Thats Plutoes Butcher bolde·
It's *Plutoes* parte to welcome him, for service done of olde.
And reason good another saide, desertes must needes bee quit,

And so they are I doe perceyve, by you in *Plutos* pit.
Some scoste & sayd, hee went for Soules, that long in *Stigion* dwelde·
And other some to preache and teache, a great opinion helde.
But in the fine a thousand thankes, they yeelded *Morpheus* there:
(And sayde) they would deserve his paines, if able that they were,
And yong man (quoth *Melpomina*) sith thou hast taken paine,
Wee doe confesse for recompence, thy debtors to remaine.
But muche I wonder howe thy witte did serve these sights to see,
Nay marvaile not (quoth *Morpheus* then) al while he was with mee.
But otherwyse in deede (not hee) nor any mortall man,
That could or might at any time, *Phlegetons* fiers scan.
Thats true, but whats his name (quoth one) hee lookes with musing moode:
He is (quoth *Morpheus*) towards you al, and sproong of *Robins* blood,
Whose painefull pen hath aye beene prest, for to advance this place,
As at these dayes, his actes full well, shal witnesse to your grace.
And certainelye his chirping tongue, delites to bawke no truth,
But plaine song partes each where doth sing, as well to age as youth.
Therfore sith I had promise made, this uglye place to see,
Mee thought a fitter man to take, I could not finde then hee.
(Quoth *Uranye*) with seemely lookes, Good sir yee saye full true.
For had you not some bodye take, no man had knowne but you.
And then your labor had been lost, which now great thanks doth crave.
Nor the reward had beene knowen, that wicked people have.

And sith you light upon our friende, ten times the gladder
   wee.
To warning of the rest we trust, these newes in Print to see.

And with these words they tooke their bookes, from *Turret*
   straight discend,
With one accord they chargde me al, to hast yet this were
   pend.
In verse (quoth *Clio*) pithilye according to your Dreame,
We charge you that to al the world, your pen doe straight
   proclaime,
And the *Rewarde of Wickednesse* your Booke shall have to
   name,
No better title can bee founde to gree unto the same.
But when I hard these woordes in deede, so full of care I
   was,
That when I should have aunswere made, no word from mee
   coulde pas.
My wits were wast, my sence was fled, and stil I stoode
   amasde,
Like Hart before the Hounde afright, or Birde in pitfall
   dasde.
And what to say I readles was, they gave so straight a
   charge,
Yet at adventure by and by, these wordes I spake at large.
Madames (quoth I) my willing mind aye alwayes yours hath
   beene,
Although the grosenesse of my head, deserv'de no praise to
   winne.
And more then twentye times ashamde, assuredlye I am,
That any of my barren workes, your learned eyes shoulde
   scan,
Apollos prudent worthie skill, nor *Pallas* active feates,
(I never knew) to promise this, how shall I pay my debtes?
My sillie eares *Minervas* voyce could never understande,
Alas good Ladies woulde you I shoulde take this worke in
   hande?
If *Caliope* rulde my pen, and did thereto agree,
Then shoulde you well and easie spie at all no fault in mee.

And sith as yet I never taste, your milke of sacred brest,
I doe beseeche you everie one, forget your last request.
And place some other in my steede, this worke in hande to take,
And so you shall your little Birde a cheerefull Robin make.
And otherwyse when all is done, for to acquite my paines,
With losse of all my labour I shall purchas *Cherils* gaines.
What, will you so (quoth one indeede,) by this what doe you meane?
Who might for shame denie us all to take so mickle paine?
What neede you to aleadge such doubts, you are to blame (quoth shee)
Who want you to assist you with, when we thus friendelie bee?
And are we not both some and all, for to erect the same?
Who ever yet tooke paine for us, but wan immortall Fame?
And then shee helde me fast bith hand, come Sisters then (quoth shee)
Come bring your keyes undoe your lockes, & let this younge man see
How we exalte the studious sorte, whose paynefull hande and quill,
Is apt at any time to yeelde their fruites unto this hill,
I hearing this, uneth one worde, durst saye but helde me still.
And countnaunce made as if I woulde consent unto their will.
And so they brought us to the place, that all the rest exceedes,
Ten times as much as in sweete May, the Cowslops stincking weede.
And meete upon the mountaine toppe, bolt up into the skies,
This noble place of endelesse fame, most curiously doth ryse,
Whose Turrets here & there doe showe the cunning workmans skill,
That first by art that statelie place began on sacred hill.

Epowdered were the Walles abroade, with stones of *Onix* kinde,
The rest was *Chrystall,* finely wrought, that like the *Orient* shinde,
Meete square it was on everye side, as could bee thought in minde·
Set out with *Phanes,* that here and there, flew up & downe the wind.
No doores but one, where on was set, nine lockes made for ye nines,
Of finest Golde, with curioust workes, outcht rounde with precious stones·
And every Sister had a key, respondent to the same,
Which by the use of Custome old, did know theyr auncient name·
To which eache Sister put her keye, abroade the Gates were cast,
They had mee come and there he holde, my Guerdon due at last.
And as wee passed through the Court, the pleasaunt house to vewe,
Amid the same I did espie, a *Laurell* where it grewe.
Wherein a thousande Birdes I thinke, or me with sweetelie voyce,
On every spray the littleones sit, and gladsomelie rejoyce.
Upon eche Laurell twigge there hange, the pennes of everie one,
Whose painefull handes their learned Muse, declared long agone·
And grav'd in gold was eche mans name, & what their travels were
For monumentes tacquite their paines, shall hang for ever there,
Thus when we had behelde at will the fashion of this tree,
These Ladies bid us yet abide a greater sight to see.
And then they brought us to a place, where all the Poetes bee,
In Pictures drawne by cunning arte, eache man in his degree.

And as their travels did appeere, to challenge prayse or fame,
Even so eache one exalted was according to the same.
Among a number some I knewe, whose workes full oft I reade,
That picturde were in livelie forme, as they had not beene deade·
The first of all, olde *Homer* sate with visage sage and sad,
Upon his head of Laurell made, a triple garlande had.
Then *Virgill* as their order is, with wan and paled lookes,
Was placed in a comelie seate, of eyther side his Bookes.
Ovid next to *Virgill sate,* as leane as hee might bee,
Whose musing moode in all respectes, did with the same agree.
And *Chawcer* for his merie tales, was well esteemed there,
And on his head as well ought best, a Laurell garland were.
All these I knewe and many moe, that were to long to name,
That for their travels were rewarde, for evermore with Fame.
And looking rounde about that house, to see and if I might
By chaunce of any countrey men of mine to have a sight:
At length I was espide there of *Skelton* and *Lydgate,*
Wager, Heywood, and *Barnabe Googe,* all these togither sate.
With divers other English men, whose names I will omit,
That in that place enjoye the like, of whome I spake not yet.
And meete behinde the doore I sawe a place where *Cherill* sate,
Arte there thought I unto my selfe? I am like to be thy mate.
By then we had behelde all this, the night was almost gone,
Therefore Ile take my leave of you (quoth *Morpheus*) every one,
Thers no remedie but depart, this youngman must away,
Beholde where *Eos* shewes hir face, and doth disclose the daye.
With al our harts these Ladies sayd: & thanks we thousands give,
And what wee may good *Morpheus* doe, its yours even while wee live.

With veyled knee unto the grounde, my leave of them I
   tooke,
Who gentlye bid mee all farewell, and chargde mee with the
   booke.
And good yong man (quoth they) take paines these few
   newes to pen,
So shalt thou earne greate thankes of us, and of all Englishe
   men.
And for our ayde bee sure of it, gainste *Zoilus* and his
   whelpes,
For to defend thy Booke and thee, wee promise heare our
   helpes.
Loe heare you see, howe wee acquite our servauntes at the
   last,
Wee cause them live, when cruell death hath take the vitall
   blast.
And here a place wee will prepare, for thee among these
   men,
That have immortall glorye wonne, by painefulnesse of pen.
At which most courteously, I cravde, and vailed with my
   knee,
And sayde good Ladies call againe, this charge if it maye
   bee.
Commit it to some other man, that hath much better skill,
And better knowth an hundreth times, to scale your learned
   Hill.
Your Honours have in Th'innes of Court, a sort of
   Gentlemen,
That fine would fit your whole intentes, with stately stile to
   Pen.
Let *Studley, Hake,* or *Fulwood* take, that William hath to
   name·
This peece of worke in hande, that bee more fitter for the
   same.
But when they hard mee speake these words, they were
   offended sore
Wee saye looke to thy charge (quoth they) and let us heare
   no more·
And then they whyrled to the Gate, away they vanisht
   straight,

Which when wee sawe wee there withall descended downe
    the hight.
So *Morpheus* brought mee home againe, from whence I came
    before,
And bade mee laye mee downe and sleepe, for I had
    traveylde   sore·
But looke (quoth he) unto thy charge: as thou wilt aunswere
    make,
Forget nothing that thou hast seene, in flaming *Stigion* Lake.
And then hee tooke his leave and went, no more I might him
    see,
But with this travaile out of hande, full sore he charged mee.
And as a man whose sillie sprightes, had wandered all the
    night,
So in a slumber waked I, and up I gat me right,
And called for the merie mates in th'evening that were there,
I mervell where they bee (quoth I) another aunswerd here.
Alas it was a death to see their lookes so deade and pale,
And how both purse, & heade of witte, were sacte and
    spoilde with ale.
Some Gaged Daggers, some their Coats, when al was   gone
    & spent
The Ale wife shee would needes bee paide, before that any
    went.
Some had surfette, some toke colde, and some for sleepe
    were lost,
(What tho) when pence were out of purse, be gon straight
    cride my host
And sende his Gestes by Crosselesie lane, and litle wittame
    home,
They neede not doubt the theefe byth way, for Money had
    they none.
Yet overnight hee that had seene, the carping of mine Host,

Howe welcome were his newcome Gestes, & how the Churle[163] could bost
Of this and that, and fill the Pots, laye Apples in the fire,
And nowe Ile drinke unto you all, thus cryed the Apple squire.
Come *Kate·* goe Wife, fill bowle againe: *Joane* looke unto the doore,
Pipe Minstrum, make us Murth a while, God sendeth al men store:
That like the *Cyrents* song, my Host playde *Synons* parte,
And made them lende theyr listening eares unto his guileful arte.
To every Feast hee biddes a Gest, fetch drinke good Dame saith hee,
And make this Gentleman some Cheere, yare welcome sir saith shee.
And thus they bid you to the Rost, and herte of all shall sit:
But or you part, I hold a crowne, theyle beate you with the spit.
I found theyr fetch, no force thought I, sith you such Cutthrotes bee,
No more then neede, or force compels, no groate you get of mee.
And there withall my Hostesse calde: I payde and got mee thence,
No favour there was to bee had, but for the litle pence.
And then I calde my Dreame to mind, whereat straight way I went,
To put in use the promise made, The time in studye spent.
Tyll I had made a finall ende, of this my little Booke,
To haste the same to Printers handes, al travailes els forsooke.
What thankes therefore I shall deserve, God knowth so doe not I.

---

[163] A Churle is a man without rank or status. OED.

But as my meaning is herein, let Fame proclaime and crye.

(Bee as bee maye) yle take my chaunce, as hap shal cast the Dice,
Sith once I knowe yet hytherto, my travaile paide the Price.

Quoth. *R. Robinson.*

BIBLIOGRAPHY

Arber, Edward, ed. *A Transcript of the Registers of the Company of Stationers of London, 1554-1640 A.D.* 5 Vols, New York, P. Smith,1950.

Bradford, Alan T. 'Mirrors of Mutability: Winter Landscapes in Tudor Poetry.' *English Literary Renaissance* 4 (1974): 3-39.

Chaucer, Geoffrey. *The Riverside Chaucer.* Ed. Larry D. Benson. 3rd ed. Oxford: Oxford University Press, 1988.

Collinson, Patrick. *The Reformation* (London: Weidenfeld & Nicolson, 2003).

Duffy, Eamon. *The Stripping of the Altars: Traditional Religion in England 1400-1580* (London: Yale University Press, 1992, 2nd ed. 2005).

Elyot, Sir Thomas. *The Book Named the Governor.* Ed. S. E. Lehmberg. London: J. M. Dent & Sons, 1970.

Foxe, John. *Acts and Monuments.* London 1563. STC 11222.
- - -. - - -. London 1570. STC 11223.
- - -. - - -. London 1583. STC 11225.

Fulwell, Ulpian. *Like will to like quoth the Devill to the Collier.* London, 1568.

Robinson, Richard. *The Rewards of Wickedness.* London 1574. STC 21121.7.

Virgil. *The Aeneid.* Trans. David West. London: Penguin Books, 1990.
- - -. The Aeneid Books I-IV. Ed. R. Deryck Williams. London: Bristol Classical Press, 1996.

Walker, Greg. *Writing Under Tyranny English Literature and the Henrician Reformation.* Oxford: Oxford University Press, 2005.

MHRA Critical Texts

This series aims to provide affordable critical editions of lesser-known literary texts that are not in print or are difficult to obtain. The texts will be taken from the following languages: English, French, German, Italian, Portuguese, Russian, and Spanish. Titles will be selected by members of the distinguished Editorial Board and edited by leading academics. The aim is to produce scholarly editions rather than teaching texts, but the potential for crossover to undergraduate reading lists is recognized. The books will appeal both to academic libraries and individual scholars.

Malcolm Cook
Chairman, Editorial Board

Editorial Board

Professor John Batchelor (English)
Professor Malcolm Cook (French) (*Chairman*)
Professor Ritchie Robertson (Germanic)
Professor Derek Flitter (Spanish)
Professor Brian Richardson (Italian)
Dr Stephen Parkinson (Portuguese)
Professor David Gillespie (Slavonic)

Published titles

1. Odilon Redon, *'Écrits'* (edited by Claire Moran, 2005)

2. *Les Paraboles Maistre Alain en Françoys* (edited by Tony Hunt, 2005)

3. *Letzte Chancen: Vier Einakter von Marie von Ebner-Eschenbach* (edited by Susanne Kord, 2005)

4. *Macht des Weibes: Zwei historische Tragödien von Marie von Ebner-Eschenbach* (edited by Susanne Kord, 2005)

5. *A Critical Edition of 'La tribu indienne; ou, Édouard et Stellina' by Lucien Bonaparte* (edited by Cecilia Feilla, 2006)

6. Dante Alighieri, *'Four Political Letters'* (translated and with a commentary by Claire E. Honess, 2007)

7. 'La Disme de Penitanche' by Jehan de Journi (edited by Glynn Hesketh, 2006)

8. 'François II, roi de France' by Charles-Jean-François Hénault (edited by Thomas Wynn, 2006)

9. Istoire de la Chastelaine du Vergier et de Tristan le Chevalier (edited by Jean-François Kosta-Théfaine, 2009)

10. La Peyrouse dans l'Isle de Tahiti, ou le Danger des Présomptions: drame politique (edited by John Dunmore, 2006)

11. Casimir Britannicus. English Translations, Paraphrases, and Emulations of the Poetry of Maciej Kazimierz Sarbiewski (edited by Krzysztof Fordoński and Piotr Urbański, 2008)

12. 'La Devineresse ou les faux enchantements' by Jean Donneau de Visé and Thomas Corneille (edited by Julia Prest, 2007)

13. 'Phosphorus Hollunder' und 'Der Posten der Frau' von Louise von François (edited by Barbara Burns, 2008)

15. Ovide du remede d'amours (edited by Tony Hunt, 2008)

16. Angelo Beolco (il Ruzante), 'La prima oratione' (edited by Linda L. Carroll, 2009)

17. Richard Robinson, 'The Rewarde of Wickednesse' (edited by Allyna E. Ward)

20. Evariste-Désiré de Parny, 'Le Paradis perdu' (edited by Ritchie Robertson and Catriona Seth)

Forthcoming titles

14. Le Gouvernement present, ou éloge de son Eminence, satyre ou la Miliade (edited by Paul Scott)

18. Henry Crabb Robinson, 'Essays on Kant, Schelling, and German Aesthetics' (edited by James Vigus)

19. A Sixteenth-Century Arthurian Romance: 'L'Hystoire de Giglan filz de messire Gauvain qui fut roy de Galles. Et de Geoffroi de Maience son compaignon' (edited by Caroline A. Jewers)

21. Stéphanie de Genlis, 'Histoire de la duchesse de C***' (edited by Mary S. Trouille)

For details of how to order please visit our website at: www.criticaltexts.mhra.org.uk

www.ingramcontent.com/pod-product-compliance
Lightning Source LLC
Chambersburg PA
CBHW060547190426
43201CB00050B/1765